VINYL JUNKIES

ADVENTURES IN RECORD COLLECTING

This one goes out to Clea Simon, for dear frienc
creative energy, and 1, 397 cups of coffee

VINYL JUNKIES: ADVENTURES IN RECORD COLLECTING.
Copyright © 2003 by Brett Milano. All rights reserved.
No part of
this book may be used or reproduced in any manner
whatsoever without written permission except in the
case of brief quotations embodied in critical articles
or reviews. For information address St. Martin's Press,
175 Fifth Avenue, New York, N.Y. 10010.

www.stmartins.com

Book design by Jonathan Bennett

Library of Congress Cataloging-in-Publication Data

Milano, Brett.
    Vinyl junkies : adventures in record collecting /
Brett Milano.
        p.   cm.
    Includes index.
    ISBN 0-312-30427-7
    1. Sound recordings—Collectors and collecting.
    I. Title.

ML111.5M53 2003
780.26'6'075—dc21

                        2003047158

D 20 19 18 17

ACKNOWLEDGMENTS

Many thanks to James and Jacqueline Milano for always insisting I'd write a book. To Pat McGrath, Jenny Toomey, Damon and Naomi, J.J. Rassler, Barbara Mitchell, Steve Wynn, Mary Lou Lord, Lauren at Rounder, and Eric at Fantagraphics for their ideas and contacts. To Peter Wolf, Thurston Moore, Peter Buck, Peter Holsapple, and Jeff Conolly for sharing their reflections and collections. To Colleen Mohyde and Michael Connor for running with it. To Julia Parker for support and sushi. And to all who tossed in ideas, shouted encouragement, or just hung out: Perry, Roy, Marlene, Jon, Zoe, Jonathan, Amy and Gary, Karen, Kevin and the Shods, Ellie, Joe and the Charms, David, Lisa, Andrew, and the LA contingent. This is also dedicated to the bands I love; especially to the Continental Drifters, Lyres, the Real Kids, Guided by Voices, Robyn Hitchcock, and the Radiators for inspirational shows. Long live the Abbey Lounge, the Middle East, and the 1369 Coffeehouse.

FOREWORD

I have been a passionate and fanatical record collector my whole life, and in the words of author Brett Milano, I am a "vinyl junkie," with an ever increasing collection of nearly 10,000 vinyl record albums and 45 RPM singles, spanning my entire lifetime. My records are my friends.

It was my mania for obscure 1960s garage/pop records that inspired me to pick up a guitar, write some songs, and form my band, The Smithereens, over twenty-three years ago. We were record collectors first; we became "serious" musicians much, much later, totally inspired by our love of collecting, and the desire to put out our own records. Why? 'Cause records were *cool*.

And they still are. I started collecting records way back in the early 1960s, when at age seven, I bought my first single, "Wipeout," by the legendary California instrumental surf combo The Surfaris, on the Fine Dot Records label. That is when the madness began and it has continued unabated ever since. I just won't listen to CDs. They don't sound right. They don't look right. They don't feel right. I believe that there is something intrinsically wrong with them. I listen to *records*. Good old noisy, loud, black vinyl 12" phonograph records. On a *turntable*. Or a *record player*. They just sound better. And there *is* a difference. I revel in the artwork, liner notes, and photographs of the colorful cardboard record sleeves that contain my records. I don't have to squint to read the liner notes. Brett Milano knows lots of people like me and understands that we are only "as sick as our secrets." He is one of us. I spent nearly twenty-three years of my life searching frantically for an unloved, unwanted, obscure, and totally uncollectible country and western album entitled *Ernest Tubb Record Shop*, simply because I liked the absurd album cover photo of good 'ole Ernest Tubb grinning from behind racks and racks of *his own records*, which he would sell at his own record store in Nashville. My quest for this miserable record had absolutely nothing to do with the music whatsoever.

But there it is. Recently, when a record dealer/collector friend of mine in the Baltimore area finally turned up a copy for me after all those fruitless years of searching for what, for me, had become a "holy grail" of sorts, I broke down in tears. Why? There is no real or defendable reason for this compulsion, this mania, this terrible malady. But in *Vinyl Junkies*, Brett Milano does seem to make sense of it all. And he brings to light a fascinating, strange, and shadowy pop subculture inhabited by obsessive record-hunting and hoarding vinyl junkies that you probably never knew existed before.

I am currently on the prowl for the mystifyingly difficult-to-find, vinyl-only release of the original soundtrack to the Vincent Price early 1970's cult horror film *The Abominable Dr. Phibes ... Why?*

Brett Milano knows why—because he is one of us. I spent many years unsuccessfully trying to track down what is perhaps the most obscure, bizarre, and elusive Elvis Presley album ever released, an early 1970s live recording on RCA Records titled *Having Fun with Elvis Onstage.*

The Smithereens were signed to the RCA Records label for a brief period in the mid-90s. I spent a considerable amount of time haunting the hallways and offices of their corporate headquarters in New York City's Times Square. One afternoon I ran into the vice president of RCA. At the end of my rope trying to find this great lost Elvis album, I begged him to go into the vaults and find me a copy. He said he would be more than happy to do so.

Then I good naturedly took him to task, letting him know in no uncertain terms that they were losing tons of potential revenue off the Elvis catalogue (Elvis is still, unbelievably, twenty-five years after his death, RCA's biggest money-earning artist) because unbelievably, RCA had let the great live Elvis album *Having Fun with Elvis Onstage* go out of print for many, many years, and that Elvis' army of fans were still clamoring for this disc, and very upset that they could not purchase it anywhere at any price. He was shocked to hear this news, and, in earnest, promised me that he would look into this matter immediately and do his best to see that the record would be reissued, and he promised to find me a copy of the record.

He scrambled to the RCA master tape vaults to unearth this potential new Elvis blockbuster, only to discover that the joke was on him.

When he listened to the master tapes of *Having Fun with Elvis Onstage* he discovered to his utter horror what I already knew; that *Having Fun with Elvis Onstage* was a "talking album only," a limited-release Colonel Tom Parker Elvis Fan Club oddity; a horrible record that featured no music, no songs, and no Elvis vocal performances at all, but instead showcased over forty minutes of inane, unfunny, incoherent, and Quaaluded-out mindless onstage in-between-song audience "raps" and ramblings by an intoxicated and druggy Elvis Presley well past his prime.

Needless to say, the vice president of RCA was not amused. He didn't get the joke, but I got the record. These are the lengths that vinyl junkies will go to. We will stop at nothing to get the records we *need*.

Brett Milano has spent his entire life writing passionately about music, musicians, and rock and roll. He is first and foremost a true music lover and, most importantly, a true fan. These are the best credentials a music writer could ever want or need or hope for. I hope that you will enjoy reading these true-life tales of record-collecting, devotion to a lost cause, obsession, and "vinyl junkie" madness with as much delight and joy as I have.

Rock and roll will stand.

—Pat Dinizio
Hollingsworth House
Scotch Plains, New Jersey
Autumn 2003

CHAPTER ONE

G*ive him* the Scythian!" shouts Monoman from across the room. Pat waves his hand with a proper flourish: Nope, I'm not ready for the Scythian yet. We'll just have to build up to it.

I'm sitting in a record-crowded apartment in the Boston suburbs, staring directly at a few hundred thousand dollars' worth of stereo equipment. Pat's stereo is nearly as eclectic as his record collection, which includes—just taking in the ones within eyesight—the Who, Doris Day, Tammy Wynette, Motorhead, Tom Jones, and Henry Mancini; this is a sensibility well beyond any standard notions of what's hip. The stereo is evidence of one man's quest for the perfect sound. The turntable is Pat's pick of the three dozen he's got in his house: suspended on air and perfectly calibrated to be vibration-free, it's designed to make sure that no small disturbances—like, say, an earthquake or a nuclear detonation—interfere with the listening experience. The turntable was made by a stereo buff in New Hampshire, the tone arm came from Germany and cost another few grand. There are pillowcases stuffed into the corners of the ceiling to keep those precious soundwaves inside. Then there's the piece of wood.

"Don't forget that piece of wood," his assistant Jeff, a.k.a. Monoman, points out. Sure enough, it's a piece of wood: cut in the shape of a beehive with a hole in the middle, it screws on top of the center hole to make sure those dreaded vibrations don't get through—according to Jeff, "The only good vibrations come from the Beach Boys." The piece of wood cost a grand on its own, but as Pat assures us, "It's a really good piece of wood."

I'd already had some of my best record-listening experiences on the crummiest stereos ever made. Stereo isn't even quite the right term—that thing I owned as a kid was more accurately a record player, a phonograph, maybe even a Victrola, but I believe the technical term we're looking for is "piece of crap": there was exactly one speaker, approximately the size of that little "O" you'd make if you closed your thumb and forefinger; and the needle tracked at something like two pounds, enough to cause instant damage to every record it touched. But it did go impossibly loud, and for ears trained on '60s AM radio, that was enough. The first record I remember playing on it was "She Loves You" by the Beatles, and it came out with that AM-radio sound: those harmonies at the start of the song sounded like a jet taking off. Which, culturally speaking, is exactly what they were. And when I later heard the same song under more desirable circumstances—on vinyl on a proper system; then on the CD reissue—it never had that compressed, unnatural sound that I always took for part of the recording.

By the time I was thirteen, I owned what I thought was a luxury stereo. It was made by Magnavox, just like my parents' TV set. The speakers folded out, and the little turntable could be closed up into the player; it was a "portable" stereo that weighed close to fifty pounds. Unlike my childhood monstrosity, this one didn't ruin your records until the second or third play. You also had the option of ruining your records instantly by stacking them on the changer, where they'd be scraped by the changer-holder on top and by other records on the bottom. By now my musical tastes had become more refined, or so I thought at the time—I was deeply into Yes, Genesis, and their progressive-rock brethren. I'm still willing to argue till closing time about those bands' musical merits, but one thing is certain: their albums were incredibly detailed, full of sonic textures and mellotron overdubs—exactly what my introverted teenage ears were looking for. At this point, records weren't something I played over dinner or with company: I wanted to *experience* all those deep, layered sounds. Armed with my Magnavox power station and a pair of weighty headphones that made your ears throb after the first album side, I listened intently enough to catch them all.

But now I'm hoping to get my mind blown in Brookline, to get the high-velocity sound I dreamed of back in my old bedroom. My guides for this trip are well known in the loose-knit community of Northeast collectors. Pat runs Looney Tunes, a used-record store that sits within the high-rent vicinity of the Berklee College of Music. The place's very existence looks like a slap at Starbuck's, Barnes & Noble, and the other upscale, uniform chains that fill up the same block. But there are enough Berklee-ites who are glad to snap up the vintage jazz and soul vinyl that clutters up the place—though they'd probably be a little spooked if they knew that their record's previous owner is likely as not to be six feet under. More than once has the widow of a collector made a call to Pat and his pickup truck; his unofficial motto is "You die, we buy." Sometimes the collections survive, but the marriage dies. Pat's been there when disgruntled wives have hit their husbands with the dreaded line, "It's me or the records." That's the cue for the husband to make his stand in front of the turntable, the wife to storm out, and Pat to go home empty-handed.

Big and gregarious, with a Southern accent that he's maintained through decades in the Northeast, Pat was drinking martinis and name-dropping the Rat Pack before it became a trend. "This is obviously the house of somebody with a problem," he notes, surveying the unfiled discs that take up every bit of floor and shelf space. But unlike the stereotypical record collector—the hyper-geeky type most recently seen in a dark attic in the film *Ghost World*—Pat doesn't shut himself away with his vinyl. He has girlfriends, eats barbeque, and has used record-collecting as an excuse to travel. For him, collecting is an intrinsic part of the good life. He's fond of quoting the line "Music frees your mind from the tyranny of conscious thought."

Monoman is unkempt, eccentric, and the leader of the best rock 'n' roll band I've ever seen. The long-standing nickname refers both to his love of monaural sound and to his relentless single-mindedness. The name has changed spellings over the years: On a 1978 album with his first band, DMZ, he was Mono Mann. More recently, he fell in love with Japanese cartoons and briefly re-christened himself Pokemonoman. His current band, the Lyres, has been together twenty-two years and shows no signs of either slowing down or changing in the slightest degree. They take their cue from '60s garage punk, the three-chord stomp that was invented by countless teens who took "Louie Louie" as their gospel. In fact, Jeff learned many Lyres's songs by scouring the globe for obscure '60s singles, paying up to a grand for an original 45. But I'd doubt that a lot of those teenage '60s bands, hormone-driven though they were, could ever match this one on an especially hot or especially drunk night. He has destroyed instruments and friendships onstage: once he fired the drummer in the middle of the show (the drummer then got pissed off enough to play the set of his life). But he's just as likely to hit you with something truly soulful; the signature Lyres song, "Don't Give It Up Now," has gotten me through more than one crisis of faith. I once saw him earnestly explain to an audience that he wasn't in it for the money: "That's why we're playing this crappy club for all of you cheap assholes!" There's been times when you'd swear that he's bypassed the tyranny of conscious thought altogether.

Today Pat's commandeered the turntable while Monoman is sinking into a couch, welcoming the chance to blow off his part-time gig cataloging records for Pat's shop. The first thing he has in store is a Doris Day record. "Why that one?" I ask. "Because it was on top of the pile, and I like it," Pat explains. First he makes sure I'm positioned in the "sweet spot," where all eight of the speakers are facing me in equal proportions. Then he advises me to lean back and keep my eyes closed. Finally he sets the needle down, making sure not to turn the volume up until it's landed. And I sit back waiting to hear the heavens open.

Instead, all I hear is Doris Day. On this particular record— a 1962 set with Andre Previn and his jazz trio—she does sound more sultry than her wholesome legend would have it. Between her alleged sexuality and the suggestive winks in a few of her hits, she could have been the Madonna of her time—go on, give "Teacher's Pet" and "Pillow Talk" another listen. Still, I'm getting no great revelations from this disc, other than that forty years of scratches add up to a whole lot of surface noise. When the drummer kicks in, it does sound as if the drumset was right there in the room. But as someone who sees live music a few times a week, I've been in enough real rooms with real drumsets that it's no big deal. And sorry, but neither is Doris Day. She may be close to sultry and modern on this record, but not quite close enough. So far I'm not impressed.

Neither is Monoman, who only looks up from his magazine long enough to note that "It's good to listen to things that aren't rock. That just makes the rock sound so much better." Like many rock-eared collectors, the three of us grew up at the mercy of our parents' musical tastes. Fortunately, mine were savvy enough to slip in the occasional gem like Ravel's "Bolero," whose primal rhythms would be the first that spoke to me—even now I'm impressed that I was able to sit through fifteen minutes of it at such a young age. For Monoman, it was show tunes: he first got the beat in "76 Trombones." From there it was '60s AM radio. "I loved the Dave Clark Five because they had the organ," he recalls. "I had a fit when I was five because I didn't get an organ for Christmas. So I ruined Christmas for everybody, and I damn well got a piano next year."

So if Doris Day can't open my ears, maybe some of that '60s music can. Pat first pulls out a cult classic, *The Turtles Present the Battle of the Bands*, and picks out the track called "I'm Chief Kamanawanalea." Yep, that one sure brings back memories of how much fun it was to shout the title at high school parties. (You can get the joke by saying "Kamanawanalea" out loud, but it's truly not worth it.) Not quite the stuff of audio nirvana, however. Okay, Pat goes for the heavy artillery: a pristine copy of the mono edition of the Beatles's *Sgt. Pepper's Lonely Hearts Club Band*. He carefully slides the

disc—with the original, sleek black U.K. Parlophone label—
out of the jacket and cues up, of all things, "She's Leaving
Home."

Not that one, I plead, I hate that song. "Wait till you hear
it in mono," he promises. "Just check out the Lennon harmonies." Nope, still hate it. But at least I've just learned why
some vinyl diehards are sticklers for mono sound: with a good
mono mix, the music sounds complete, as if it's all being
pumped from the same heart. And John's chorus counter-
points are indeed louder in this version, always a plus. None
of which is enough to keep this tearjerker of Paul's from being one of the small handful of Beatles songs that I just can't
deal with.

Mono Beatles albums have a cachet in the collector's market, in part because they're so scarce—stereo was no longer
just a luxury item by the time the Beatles split up—and, because at this point, any newly-mined variation on a Beatles
record is to be treasured. In the case of *Sgt. Pepper*, there are
certain vocal bits—like a spoken rant by Paul right before "A
Day in the Life"—that got mixed into oblivion on the stereo
version. Beyond the collector's value, vinyl junkies detect a
richness and warmth in mono records of this era, something
to bring you closer to the sound of the period, to hearing the
record in its original context. For a time Monoman refused
to listen to anything else, and he still spends an inordinate
amount of time and money questing for original editions of
'60s singles, and he won't allow his Lyres to perform a '60s
song unless an original copy is sitting in his collection. Most

recently a European dealer sent him a tape of a little-known single and he fired back three hundred dollars for it—even though the music itself was already there on the tape. But it's about something more than just hearing a song: "Those original pressings are what you need to bring you closer to the original event."

So are collectors just looking for a great musical experience like everyone else, though maybe with more fervor? Not quite. Because there's an element of fetishism in this as well, and it gets unleashed when Pat pulls out that vintage *Pepper*. Ninety percent of the people in the world would register an album cover they've seen a million times and move on. Not the case here: the picture may be the same, but the plastic lamination is different. "Whoa!" Monoman leaps from his chair. "I've never seen that one before." "Pretty unusual, isn't it?" Pat says. "The cover doesn't feel as heavily embossed as usual." Here's where we get into the deep details. Old Bob Dylan records, for example, have distinguishing marks on the labels. You can spot a first pressing by an indent around the edge of the label itself (and collectors swear you'll be rewarded with a better-sounding copy). The date of this *Pepper* is more elusive: maybe in the '70s, when some new cardboard stock came into the pressing plants? But doesn't the record itself sound closer to that desirable first pressing? The mystery isn't about to get solved, and the original owner isn't around to clear it up. When you start wondering about the personal history of a disc you've just acquired, you're getting close to the point of no return.

Time is wasting, however, and I still haven't had my mind blown. "Give him the Scythian!" Monoman yells. Not quite. Pat has one more trick up his sleeve. This time it's Louis Armstrong. The disc is *Satchmo Plays King Oliver*, a 1962 release on the Audio Fidelity label. It's theoretically from the dark ages, when stereo recording was still in its infancy. But damn, now we're talking revelation. Every note on this thing is beautifully vivid, and it doesn't hurt that the music (the New Orleans standard "St. James Infirmary") is stellar. My memories of a lesser Louis Armstrong doing "Hello Dolly" or the sentimental "What a Wonderful World" (a song I'd rank down there with "She's Leaving Home") are melting away by the minute. And here I'm learning one of the secrets: that good stereo sound is a psychedelic experience. I'm not just seeing Satchmo's horn, I'm seeing the shape of the notes and the color of the sound. When he sings, I'm looking deep down into his throat while the drums and bass push me from behind. So now I understand why a lot of record collectors don't do drugs—when they crank that stereo up, they're already doing one.

Every vinyl junkie has a moment like this, when the sound hits you between the eyes and you're hooked for life. Pat got the rush when "Be My Baby" by the Ronettes was blaring from a car radio. Producer Phil Spector made that record to be overwhelming—with its massive drums and heavenly choir—and in Pat's case (and that of the Beach Boys's Brian Wilson, who also loved the record) it did the trick. As for Monoman, he gets reinitiated every time he discovers a new medium. Lately his drug of choice is reel-to-reel tapes, the ones that were issued in the '60s and only played in high-class bachelor pads. "It's the Hugh Hefner thing. Those tapes were the high-end item, the compact disc of their day. The goal is to get as close to the master tape as possible. That's where the reel tapes bring me, and the turntable is another path."

It's getting late, however, and though Louis Armstrong started me down the path, I've still got a foot in the real world. So now it's time to pull out the heavy artillery, as they prepare to give me the Scythian. That would be the "Scythian Suite" by Prokofiev, but not just any copy. This is the 1957 recording by Antal Dorati and the London Symphony Orchestra on the Mercury label—one of the first stereo recordings ever issued. The legend "Mercury Living Presence" blazes proudly across the cover; the same design is still there on the current compact-disc edition. But we're looking to get close to the master tape and deep into the music, and the preferred path is that original 1957 pressing, made while the master tape was likely still throbbing. Pat produces the item from the middle of a stack, in a dark corner of his collection. "Is that a real one?" asks Monoman, raising his eyes. Pat nods his head with proper gravity. This is starting to look like the glow-box scene from *Pulp Fiction*—hell, maybe a pristine copy of the "Scythian Suite" was the box's mysterious contents.

"Just feel how round that edge is," notes Pat, running a finger around the LP's circumference. "Yeah, it's the real deal," Monoman nods. The glossy laminated cover is also studied, and the disc's runout groove is inspected for the distinguishing mark: the letter "I" stamped into a small circle.

That stands for Indianapolis, which means the record was stamped at that city's RCA plant—in other words the record is like any good fix, clean and uncut by cheap additives. As Pat bears it to the turntable, Monoman gives the music some perspective: "Those Scythians, man, they were fuckin' pagans! Human sacrifices, you name it." I have been warned.

Maybe Pat's discreetly jacked up the bass and treble, maybe he's slipped something in my tea. In any case, the Scythian starts and all hell breaks loose. A big unearthly screech—that's the strings making fire-and-brimstone noises. A roll of thunder from dangerously close—that's the orchestral bass drums. "AAAH! We're all gonna fuckin' die!"—that's Monoman feeling the spirit, running around the room with hair shaking and shirttail flying. If Prokofiev wasn't aiming for exactly that response, I'm sure that whoever engineered the record was. The roller-coaster construction of the piece only helps the effect: there are a few moments of deceptive calm before the thunder starts up again, this time with added gongs. "That's it, that's heavy metal!" is Monoman's reaction, his shouts becoming a perfectly fitting vocal part. "Hey, Led Zeppelin—you suck!"

This is where the addiction starts: when the music and the sound get so beautifully overwhelming that you wouldn't mind devoting a chunk of your life to more of the same. For now, the purple vacuum tubes are starting to calm down, and any more music would be overkill. Pat can take pride in making another convert, and Monoman can come down off his vinyl high. "The Scythian, man. Can't get enough of it."

Chapter Two

Why We Collect
(their effort)

33 ⅓

I'm not a collector, I'm a friggin' archivist," Monoman tells me soon after, spreading a bunch of CDs on the table in front of him to make his point. I'm trying in vain to play devil's advocate, suggesting that he really doesn't need as many mid-'60s, European punk singles as he's got. Maybe I can make him see the error of his ways. Or, at least, maybe he'll consider selling a few of them to me. No luck.

"My trip is about using the music," he explains, choosing a CD to use next. "I don't believe in the idea of ownership—hey, we're all gonna die someday so you don't own that record, you just get to use it for awhile. There is no joy in ownership, the joy comes when you play the record. The hair stands up on the back of your neck and that's it, that's what you're living for. So my track record can show that I've used the music, and so I can sleep at night."

Another musician who doubles as a collector, Sonic Youth guitarist Thurston Moore, is also something of a friggin' archivist. "When you're a collector, you're creating order out of this chaotic information," Moore tells me. "That's necessary in a way, and it caters to creative impulses. There's something I really like about the archival nature of it—you're gathering information that falls below the radar, so it becomes less ignored. That's why I separate myself from, say, Beatles collectors. Collecting mainstream material is a different thing, more like collecting toys, more object-oriented. I'm more interested in defending the cultural value of music that's not allowed into the mainstream. That's more of a renegade practice."

His own collecting has gone through different phases. "All of the rock stuff I own, either vintage or modern, was collected sporadically between bouts of being completely destitute through the '80s. In the '90s I was finally able to make enough money to buy records, by then I wanted things that were even more subterranean in the culture. Right now I'm getting a lot of English psychedelic folk stuff, that's become a really interesting genre to me. Many collectors are artist-specific, but I'm just as likely to go by labels—I like discovering the independent labels of the '60s, because there was a whole scene that existed concurrently with the major labels, before the majors put a stranglehold on the whole culture. You get a jazz label like Impulse! in the '60s, and that's something that collects really well, because they were seriously into design. They were just so amazing-looking."

Love for the music, love for the artifact, the thrill of the chase: those are the three elements that turn a garden-variety music lover into a vinyl junkie. Like many collectors, Monoman is on an eternal mission: There's always something out there that he hasn't yet got. And he's sealed his lifestyle forever by choosing those '60s singles as his main passion: those aren't hanging around in just any closet, or even any record store. There may be two copies sitting in Holland somewhere. Your job: find them.

Right now he's chasing down an EP by Tony Jackson, whom history remembers (if at all) as the original lead singer of the Searchers, of "Needles & Pins" fame (as fate would have it, bad-boy Jackson got kicked out of the band just before they cut that song). When Jackson recorded his solo EP in 1966, he wouldn't have guessed that a bad xerox of the picture sleeve would be hanging on a refrigerator in Cambridge, Massachusetts some thirty-six years later. Barely a few hundred people bought the record in the first place; hardly anyone has bothered tracking down Jackson himself lately, much less his record. "Somebody in America has to own this record," Monoman says. "And I'm convinced that it has to be me."

When and if he finds this record, he gets more than a slab

of vinyl, more even than bragging rights. He gets to experience whatever the vinyl holds, to know exactly what the music—which he already owns on a cassette dub—sounds like in its original pressing. He's collected many such experiences over the years: did you know that the original single of "96 Tears" by ? and the Mysterians, on the regional Pa-Go-Go label, was longer than the Cameo/Parkway version that everybody's heard? Monoman does. "There's a lot of mysteries trapped in those grooves, and I get joy out of learning those mysteries. If I can learn one thing a year, that's great."

They were the same mysteries that hooked me into collecting. When I was a kid I remember staring at records for hours, trying to figure out where the music was. I figured out early on that it had something to do with vibrations and amplification, once I realized that the Beatles weren't really sitting inside that big gramophone waiting to break into song, at exactly the right spot, whenever I dropped the needle. Beyond that it was all a mystery, but as I held this thing in my hand I'd try to figure out how it could make the songs materialize out of thin air. How were these flat plastic slabs able to do such great things? How come they all looked the same and all sounded different?

I learned to read by memorizing record labels; I'm sure that "Elvis's Golden Records" were three of the first words I learned to recognize in print. That was the first album I remember loving—at four years old I was cute enough to get away with stealing it from my older sister—and it had my favorite label as well: that old, chocolate-brown RCA one, with the little dog staring into that contraption on top. The dog's being there made perfect sense to me: "Hound Dog" was the first and best song on the record, right? But I always felt a little sorry for that mutt as well. No matter how intently he faced forward and stared into that horn, whenever you played the record he always spun backwards.

Even if I didn't love the music, the records were fascinating in themselves. The labels were all brightly colored and full of space-age squiggles that made it clear how much of a technical marvel this was. The Capitol album label, with its colors on the edge that blurred into an endless rainbow when you played it; the cherry-red Columbia, with its stylized antenna; the rarefied gold-and-silver Warner Brothers designs—all were enough to make you feel that you were participating in some great experiment when you played one. My favorite design, appropriately enough, was on some long-gone label called Design, which specialized in cheap-shot easy-listening versions of the hits of the day, as performed by some anonymous orchestra—my parents' chosen alternative to "She Loves You" (whose original U.S. incarnation on Swan sported an inappropriately blah, flat-black label). Design's music was pretty grating—in fact, one quasi-Dixieland novelty, "Autumn in Azusa" by Jerry Colonna, was awful enough to stay lodged in my subconscious to this day—but it was nearly worth it to watch the multicolored, interlocking triangles of its label spin round. Jerry Colonna, if you're out there, can I have my money back?

The urge to collect records begins with the fascination

with the record as an object, going beyond simple appreciation of the music. Any music fan could get to know a song
on a favorite 45, a bigger fan might risk playing the B-side.
But a vinyl junkie would make discoveries from the record
itself. Compact discs will remain a sticking point for collectors, but you don't have to be one of those vinyl snobs—the
kind who think that digital sound is flat and heartless—to
appreciate that playing a record is a whole different experience. Placing the needle in the groove is a physical act—
maybe a sexual one, if you really want to stretch the metaphor—and it's just not the same as pressing the button on
your CD player, where you can't even see what's going on.
And even though they're more high-tech, CDs just aren't as
mysterious. There's a computer-age explanation for why that
digital sound gets reproduced, just as there's a computer-age
explanation for everything.

Record collecting itself has changed shape in recent decades. During the '70s, it was necessary for any serious music
fan to be something of a collector, since so many important
albums—by the likes of John Coltrane, the Velvet Underground, and even the Beach Boys—were either out of print
or available in truncated, shoddily packaged or badly mastered editions (the Beach Boys albums with songs taken off
them, or the first Velvets with the banana skin permanently
pressed on, rank with the dregs of the era). Meanwhile a few
mavericks, like artist Robert Crumb and his crew, were
scouring the country for 78s that had been languishing in
garages and basements. At the same time, the punk revolution was rediscovering the thrill of the instant collectible—

45s with exclusive songs, picture discs and colored vinyl. By the mid-'80s, the twelve-inch rap and disco single was proving just how much loud bass could be captured on a vinyl slab. This was the vinyl era's last real moment of glory.

There are certainly exceptions, and it's safe to say that every halfway desirable record out there has a collector who wants it. But most of today's collectors are running after music that's barely two decades old. Punk and rap singles from the '80s have largely replaced vintage jazz and R&B as the most sought-after items. "Early doo-wop 45s and 78s were the Holy Grail of collecting during the '70s," recalls former *Goldmine* editor Jeff Tamarkin. "Now you can barely give that stuff away. Even Elvis seems to be dying as a collectible artist. That's partly because the people who would collect that kind of music are getting older and have different responsibilities. If you're twenty-two and just getting into collecting, you're not going to be into that."

Today, nearly everything that's ever been on vinyl is on CD somewhere, and available from eBay and its clones (I'm partial to the set-sale site gemm.com, where you may have to pay more but are spared the bidding). The amount of time for the average treasure hunt has been cut down drastically: I recently developed an uncanny craving for *A Bag of Soup*, the Soupy Sales album on Motown—to my mind, the cultural accident of the pie-faced comic being on the same label as Diana Ross and Marvin Gaye was too much to resist. I cruised the Web for a few minutes, and had it within days. One of these years, I might even play it.

Neither development has made record collectors any

scarcer—though the eBay phenomenon means that many collectors, a secretive group to begin with, can do a lot of their hunting in private. But it's also made collectors even hungrier for the peak experience of finding something desirable tucked away in a box in someone's attic. And the ubiquity of CDs has only created new appreciation for the aesthetic perfection of vinyl.

"*A record* is that object that you can hold and watch and learn from," notes Miriam Linna, who's made a few of those objects herself. She was the original drummer for the Cramps, and today runs the independent Norton label. "Look at the label, it's got all that information that somebody wanted to give you. There's the names of the people who wrote the song, the names of who published it, and maybe where the record comes from—if you don't find that one, it's just another mystery to solve. And the record, that's a couple minutes of instant gratification; it's as good as a good cup of coffee. And it's a common denominator, you want people to be clued in. You play someone a great record and they don't react to it, you know it's time to get them out of your house."

Besides, she says, a record has the human touch embedded in the grooves, the stamp of someone who once believed in it. (True, a CD has that, too, but it's easier to imagine those digital discs being untouched by human hands.) "When I grew up, I always had the attitude that you had to be good to make a record. In the early days of rock 'n' roll, you couldn't just buy a pressing plant if you were a teenager. It was all about making a racket for your friends and doing something that would be offensive to adults. So I thought it was a great mystery how those records got made. Even if it was on a smaller label, somebody, somewhere, decided that person was good. They could make a record, and that was a fabulous, important thing. Now I know how they're made: some piece of black rubber gets thrown on, then a stamper stamps 'em out and trims them. Seeing a record made is the coolest thing because you're seeing something that can actually change the quality of somebody's life, or change their mood, or make a chemical difference in their bloodstream. It's a really heavy deal when you think about it."

A long cool woman in her forties, Linna radiates enough energy to put many teenagers to shame—so much for the stereotype of geeky, mild-mannered collectors. "It's not about being a geek, it's about being mental," she says—that term of course being a high compliment in rock 'n' roll circles. "If you're a record collector, you're looking for the source of something that's great. If you go to a record show, you see some really mild-mannered guys there with their collections, maybe they run labels. But to me that's more mental than some guy walking around with leather, tattoos, and his hair sticking out."

Like any kind of collecting, record collecting represents a small, irrational stab at immortality. If you've bothered to accumulate all that vinyl, you must believe on some deep, optimistic level that you're really going to have a use for all of it. How else to explain the reluctance of most collectors to purge the sillier things they've acquired? To name one of the thoroughly useless items in my collection, I can tell you that I'm holding onto *Bad Animals* by Heart for shock value, or because nobody's ever going to buy it from me, or because they made some good albums (of which this isn't one). But the fact is that I really believe that someday I'll have the forty-five disposable minutes in my life that this record was just made to fill. And I always have the luxury of getting up, putting the thing on, and proving myself right.

Such is the dual nature of record collecting: it's pathetic and it's glorious. Yes, you're filling your life with extraneous stuff—vinyl and aluminum slabs that will never transport you back to youth, or get you a hot date, or bring Nick Drake back to life. If you're far enough along, you've probably got a handful of things you forgot you even own, and a few that your ex-girlfriend misfiled ten years ago. Somebody will unearth those discs one day, and it might not be you. Never mind that you can't take it with you, you can't even find a tidy place to put it in the meantime.

That's the egalitarian aspect of collecting, in that rich and poor collectors devote the same space to their collections—namely, whatever space they've got. In either case, you've made a decision to accumulate. And somewhere along the line, you lost the possibility of keeping track of it all. Thus it's always a collecting rite of passage when you first buy something twice by accident.

Not surprisingly, some musicians who collect tend to be less organized about it. "I've got few dozen boxes of rare punk singles sitting in my basement," admits Steve Turner, guitarist for the pioneering Seattle grunge band Mudhoney. "They're not sealed; they're lucky if I get them back into the sleeves. For every good record I've got, I buy twenty shitty ones. I go to thrift stores, a lot of times I'll buy a pile of things just for the covers. It got pretty random. When Mudhoney was touring I'd grab the phone book, look up the record stores, and hop in a cab. Touring would have been pretty boring otherwise. If someone told me a store sucked I'd probably go there—that would mean it hadn't been scoured as clean as the other stores."

'70s and '80s punk singles are Turner's specialty, and he wound up perfecting one shopping tactic: "I know how record store people work—if they don't know what something is, they'll just ignore it. So let's say I'm poking around an attic of a store, and I find something great. I'll stick those at the bottom of the pile and put something crappy on top—say, a single by Generation X [Billy Idol's first band, not quite revered by punk scholars]. They'll see my pile, say, 'The one on top is ten dollars, but the rest are a buck.' So I'll put the Generation X one back and take the rest."

Turner would be hard-pressed to tell you exactly what he owns, but he can look around his bedroom and survey the thrift store finds from the past few weeks. Since he's in the middle of recording an acoustic album, he's been on a Joan Baez bender. "That stuff isn't really worth anything, so I picked up loads of it. It's starting to make sense to me now that I'm getting into middle age. I've been known to steal riffs off records that I've bought—most of them, in fact—but

I can always steal something that the other guys in Mudhoney haven't heard, so they'll play something different along to it." Turner's collecting does have a methodical side—he's especially into the *Killed By Death* series, a semi-bootleg CD compilation of rare punk singles, and tracking the original copies of those singles down. But he also loves to simply have loads of vinyl lying around. When the name of another prominent guitarist, collector, and Seattle resident, R.E.M. member Peter Buck, comes up, Turner's mock-pissed off response is, "I've seen his collection and I've got more records than him, dammit! I mean, they may not be good records, but at least I've got 'em."

Representing the more methodical collectors is Geoffrey Weiss of Los Angeles. He's also an industry veteran who's done A&R at the Warner Brothers, A&M, and Hollywood labels. Weiss has a separate building to hold the 100,000 discs in his collection, not counting the ones that are still hanging out in his parents' house. His love of music grew at about the same rate as a need to accumulate and catalog it. "When I was ten I decided that I had to buy all the Beatles's records. I was under the impression that I was preserving them for posterity, because such important things were going to be lost." He's become something of a punk and psychedelic specialist, citing his discovery of the Ramones and the '60s reissue series *Chocolate Soup for Diabetics* as pivotal events. But his hunger goes beyond the constraints of those categories. "When people ask me what I collect, I just say 'everything.' I'm not in this to accumulate the most records—it's more that I just want to have all the music that I love."

But for a true collector, the buzz comes from owning a record—playing it is something extra. "My records would have value to me if I was deaf," says Weiss, known as one of the most devoted collectors in the music industry. Not only won't he have time to play all his records, his kids and grand-kids won't either, even if they started right away. "Of course, I get more from them not being deaf. But I get pleasure from looking at the covers, making connections between the cred-its. It isn't just what's in the grooves, it's the whole thing—what's on the label, what's in the dead wax." And he insists that the highest quality experiences come from tracking down the original object. "Take a record like *Heavy Petting* by Dr. Strangely Strange," he says, naming an eccentric Irish folk-rock band, greatly beloved by the few dozen people who've heard of them. "It was on the Vertigo label with that die-cut cover, the custom inner sleeve that matches the label. There's a tactile aspect of that, that's very hard to reproduce; I doubt that anyone's even tried. Or *Once Upon a Twilight* by the Twilights—they were an Australian band with great, me-lodic, pop/psychedelic songs, and their album had this in-credibly ugly pop-up in the gatefold. There's something magical about seeing one that's not a reproduction—the way it was intended, flaws and all. There's no experience you can have with that record that's anything like taking it out of the original cover and putting it on the turntable."

On a more emotional level, collecting puts you into a world that you can control; each record is a small piece of emotional essence that can be plugged into your life. San Francisco musician Roger Manning has been into records all his life, but it took an emotional shakeup, the 1994 breakup of his band Jellyfish, to push him over the line. Along with vinyl, he was into collecting vintage gear. "I really didn't want that band to break up, so it was traumatic for me when it did—a very draining, very psychotic time. And now that I look back on it, that's when I started collecting like a maniac; I realize that it was self-medicating. I started looking for whatever vintage instruments I could afford with my savings, and I started getting pretty good at finding them. And that started taking my mind off the daily blows—devoting my time to this obsession. On some level I was doing fine as long as I could be better at the hunt than the next guy—I was gonna be the one that found that old synthesizer, that vintage piece of vinyl. The escapism of that search wound up buffering the pain of what was really going on in my life."

In his case, collecting was also a regression to childhood, since some of his favorite teenage memories revolved around record-scavenging. "I grew up in a suburb of the Bay Area. My friends and I would save our money over the course of the week, then we'd take a bus to Telegraph Avenue in Berkeley; an area that has five or six used record stores. Then it would be a free-for-all—we'd just raid the dollar section and start pulling out whatever we could. We liked jazz, so we'd see a Herbie Hancock record and say, 'This guy played with Miles, I hear that he's cool.' Then we got into progressive rock and new wave, which were nearly as obscure as jazz." No surprise that Jellyfish itself was much liked by collectors with a pop bent: the band's two albums were even packaged to look like '70s albums, released on vinyl with gatefolds. "What really got me was the smell of the records I grew up with—maybe it was the pressing plant they used, for some reason records on the Casablanca label had a smell that blew our minds—when you smell that, it brings you right back to childhood. So we wanted to find a way to make our records smell that way, but of course nobody at our label knew what the hell we were talking about."

It might be a passing phase or a permanent persuasion, but collecting does require a leap of faith; the belief that some emotional core can be found in those grooves—admittedly a tall order when you're talking about Soupy Sales on Motown. One of the few lapsed collectors I've encountered, novelist Pagan Kennedy, puts this into perspective. "I think that as Americans we can get sidetracked . . . into stuff," she says, her thick glasses and fast head movements giving her the air of a sharp urban cynic. "The paradox of collecting is that people are trying to put something in a cage. I used to get a lot of records; I thought of it as my escape from the prevailing culture. Then one day I woke up and said, hey look at me—here I am obsessively going to yard sales, just like all those people going to the mall! I'm still surrounded by all this . . . this stuff! It's the same revelation I had about marijuana years ago, that if one puff makes me happy, it doesn't mean that two are going to make me happier."

Yet the album that indoctrinated her was the same one that won many collectors over: the *Pebbles* series of '60s punk reissues. "Someone played it for me in college and I'm feeling—Oh, my God. This is good music, and it's music that I never knew existed. It was what I wanted to hear all my life, it was amazing, and it pointed the way to some vision of life that I couldn't even name. But it was only a glimpse; that's me, and that's what's important to me. And I've been struggling in my life to remember that the feeling isn't something you can buy: The thing you love is ephemeral, that little evanescent pleasure you can get. It speaks to some world that you want to be in. And you're not going to get into that world by finding the B-side of some Italian single. You'll probably find that there's a reason it was a B-side."

What she says makes perfect sense, but the appeal of collecting is that it doesn't necessarily make sense. On some level, there are times when you've just got to be mental.

CHAPTER THREE
IT'S A SEROTONIN THING

*I*n *psychiatric* circles, the expression "going mental" is generally frowned upon. So, to some extent, is collecting, which is seen as a fairly benign disorder.

According to Alen Salerian, director of the Washington Psychiatric Center, the need to collect anything stems from a serotonin deficiency. Serotonin is the enzyme that controls worries; with too little of the former you get too much of the latter. "It's a form of addiction, if you want to call it that. The current thinking in neuroscience is that people with serotonin deficiencies are much more driven to compulsions, including the compulsion to collect. Various life events may disturb you and prompt that compulsion."

Serotonin deficiency is the condition that Prozac and

other antidepressant drugs are commonly prescribed to treat. Those with lower levels of serotonin are believed to have higher appetites—whether for sex, alcohol, gambling or original copies of the "Scythian Suite." A study by the National Institute of Alcohol Abuse and Alcoholism found that rhesus monkeys with lower serotonin levels were also more likely to demonstrate violent or dangerous behavior. No word on whether the monkeys preferred to collect vinyl or CDs.

So an ideal serotonin balance can be tougher to obtain than, say, a still-sealed copy of *Nazz Nazz* on red vinyl. The good news, however, is that this condition is more common among creative types. "Many people with creative genes also suffer from various neurological disorders; you can be Mozart and still be bipolar," says Salerian. "There is a very close link between creativity and dysfunction of the nervous system— it's part of a mood disorder package that artistic people have a higher chance of suffering from. As for collecting, the line I would draw is whether a person's life is compromised because of this habit. You can gamble without being a pathological gambler. But if something like collecting interferes with your ability to function effectively, then it's a problem that should be addressed."

Or, to put it another way, "At least they're not as bad as Trekkies." This contribution comes from Jeff Tamarkin, who saw his share of crazed collectors as an editor of *Goldmine*. "What always amazed me was how a certain kind of obsessiveness took over that went way beyond even caring about the music. You start off because you like what's on the records, and it becomes something else along the way. I saw people that would buy a record and never play it, and that struck me as pretty odd. Of course, the records they prized the most were the ones in mint condition, and you can only keep it mint if you don't play it. So people would buy a record, wrap it in plastic and mount it. The people I thought had the best attitude were the ones who didn't mind buying a record that was covered with scratches, as long as they liked the tune." Tamarkin points out that he's sold original singles by the infamous gutter punk GG Allin. Before his fatal overdose, Allin was notorious for flinging abuse, and various bodily materials, at his audiences; I can vouch that he once chugged Ex-Lax before a Boston gig. Nowadays his records go for hundreds of dollars on eBay: the music may be filthy, but the vinyl is still pristine.

There's a thin but definite line between serious music fans and collectors, but the two worlds will always intersect. If you discovered garage rock from the Nuggets or Pebbles series and were driven to hear more, if you bought a Velvet Underground album before R.E.M. or Kurt Cobain told you to, or if you even buy vinyl in the twenty-first century, then you're on the road to collecting—you're looking for something that the charts and the chainstores won't give you. But when you start thinking seriously about methods of alphabetizing, or start worrying about preserving records instead of collecting them, then you've entered the realm of the true collector.

The choice of music may be different, but the obsession is the same, and collecting punks have more in common with jazz and classical snobs than they might realize: in each case, it's about holding onto something beyond the music. Other theorists tell us that the idea of collectors as "anal" has some basis in clinical fact. Otto Fenichel writes, in *The Psychoanalytic Theory of Neuroses*, "The anal retention, which always contains the two components, fear of loss and enjoyment of a new erogenous pleasure, may also be displaced to another object. Cupidity and collecting mania have their correlating determinants in the infantile attitude toward feces." We won't even venture to guess what the notoriously scatological GG Allin would have done with this one.

Elaborating further, the psychologist Werner Muensterberger poses that the urge to collect may stem from early childhood traumas. In his book *Collecting: An Unruly Passion*, he writes: "Provoked by early, possibly unfavorable conditions or the lack of affection on the part of not-good-enough mothering, the child's attempt toward self-preservation quickly turns to some substitute to cling to. Thus, he or she has a need for compensatory objects of one or the other kind. This can also be interpreted as a self-healing attempt. . . . To put it another way, such a person requires symbolic substitutes to cope with a world he or she regards as basically unfriendly, even hazardous."

Pat, the store owner and collector, says that his mother influenced his collecting in a more direct way. "I always told her she was to blame, since she was a music lover who accumulated a lot of records. Or at least that's what I thought, that I was using her as a role model. It was only after I told her that, that she said: 'You know, I didn't have more than maybe one hundred records. I never dreamed you'd go so berserk.' "

Muensterberger goes on to offer a role model that record collectors may be more comfortable with: "There are, to be sure, all sorts of collectors and facets of collecting. While one would not normally think of the infamous Spanish nobleman Don Juan Tenorio as a collector, did he not in fact 'collect' the chaste young maidens he seduced one after the other?"

Intentionally or not, Muensterberger has just hit on one trick of successfully living the collector's life—to embrace the Don Juan model, spiritually if not literally. In other words, to treat collecting as a safe outlet for promiscuity, to follow crushes and make conquests. And you don't have to unload the old passions when you move on—you can just file them in the basement, and maybe rekindle the affair someday. "I'd get rid of the ones I'll never play again, but Lord knows which ones those are," says Pat, echoing a sentiment familiar to collectors. "It's good to have them there whenever I want them. And it's a comfort to know that I can read or think about something, then go down to the basement and hear it. That's immediate gratification. For some people, the drug is in the purchase; it speaks to some sense of order that they have. Some relate to records as an artifact of an era. And, of course, for some collectors, the drug is being able to find something rare, and then to lord it over everybody else."

In that sense, collecting—as Salerian notes above—is like many other drugs: not necessarily something that needs to be avoided, just something that you need to know how to handle and live with comfortably. And that includes the knowledge that you can't embrace collecting without succumbing just a little to the X factor, that urge to go mental. Pat recalls the time that some Japanese friends stayed in his house, and voiced concern over how close one of his floors was to collapsing. "They saw that I sleep right below one of the record storage rooms, and they saw how easy it would be to get crushed by records if the ceiling ever caved in during the night. And I just thought, 'Well, you're right. But wouldn't that be an honorable way to go?' "

Serotonin, anybody?

CHAPTER 4

THE LURE OF VINYL

Compact discs are a lot like the Republican Party: they may have all the power but if you move in certain circles, you can't find anybody who actually voted for them. There's a lot to love about the silver discs: they're modern, they're portable and, to put this in technical jargon, they kick a lot of butt—nobody ever woke up their neighborhood by driving down the street blasting a vinyl record.

Yet serious record collectors are, for the most part, record collectors. The issue of whether records or CDs sound better can be debated endlessly—it has been, and it will be. While a case could be made for either sound, there's something about vinyl that endears it to collectors. It's a more sensual medium: you can have more fun holding it, and watch it while it's playing. If you're old enough, it's always going to trigger memories of prying your favorite LP out of the sleeve for the first time, discovering the surprises on the label and the inner sleeve. And maybe it's just that a record has more style—the "Hugh Hefner thing," as Jeff put it. Yes, John Travolta clicked on a CD player before his romantic interlude with Uma Thurman during *Pulp Fiction*—and was rewarded with Urge Overkill's sleek, modern cover of a Neil Diamond song—but just look at how well that encounter turned out.

"The romance of vinyl is that it's more textural, tangible," says engineer Bill Inglot, who's best known as a remastering expert for CDs. "All CDs have that plastic cover, and they basically all look the same. CDs are like sex with a condom."

Another industry veteran, Bob Irwin, runs the Sundazed label, which reissues lost '60s classics on both CD and vinyl. And he says that vinyl has made a comeback since the turn of the millennium, at least among the collectors who love his label. "In the past two years our vinyl shares have spiked over 35 percent; the romance of holding a 45 or an album is coming back. You can't watch two hours of primetime TV without seeing something like a car commercial, where the needle drops into a groove."

Most of all, LPs appeal to people like Clark Johnson, a self-proclaimed vinyl snob who amasses records and stereo equipment in his Boston area apartment and who treats every play like an experience to be savored. "I really like CDs," he notes soon after I step in the door. "They make good coasters." Sure enough, he hands me a beer and invites me to plop it down on the lonely CD sitting without a sleeve on his kitchen table.

When people draw generalizations about record collectors—that they're anal, middle-aged guys with too much time on their hands—Johnson is the kind of guy they're talking about, and darn proud of it. And he's the kind of person who can make you wonder whether you've been taking a simple experience like playing records for granted. Balding and professorial, wearing a well-used flannel shirt, he speaks in a booming voice that would sound equally at home in a lecture hall or on AM radio. Looking around his kitchen I see evidence of a lifetime of collecting, and I haven't even gotten to the records yet. Just the beer bottles that line every available bit of wall space: all exotic, all imports or microbrews and, shamefully enough, all still full. Though I spent a few hours at his house, we never reached the point where he actually played any records—that isn't something you do with a stranger, the first time around. "That's what radio is for, if you want to listen to something in the background," he says. "But if I want to listen to a Mahler symphony, I want to *listen* to it. If you go to a concert, what else would you be doing?"

As a kid, he built turntables out of tinker toys, before he graduated to taking apart and re-assembling real ones. He still keeps the first record he ever owned, a disc of his own voice made in one of those old amusement-park booths. Growing up in the '50s he once got to see Buddy Holly perform, and even holds a ticket for the concert that Holly would have played in Iowa if his plane hadn't crashed the night before.

Most of Johnson's life since then has been spent in pursuit of that perfect sonic wave. He once owned a low-profit business he dubbed the Listening Studio, designed to let his fellow sound aficionados test-drive their vinyl on high-end equipment. The suburban Boston house where he now lives easily has a half-million dollars of music in it. Once you get past the kitchen—a room kept music-free for those moments when one needs to rest and refuel—the vinyl covers nearly every room of the three-story house. Climbing the stairs, I nearly misstepped and trashed a rare Japanese pressing of *Sgt. Pepper's Lonely Hearts Club Band.*

The top floor houses the most valuable of his albums. I can't confirm his estimate that there's $20,000 worth in this room alone, but it is an impressive batch of first-edition classical LPs from the '50s and '60s. The hallowed "Scythian Suite" is one of the first things I spot, along with an Offenbach recording by Arthur Fiedler & the Boston Pops—notable, he says, as the first classical LP that RCA ever produced. "This is where I keep the records that sound good," he says, and points to a darker corner. "And over there is where I keep the records that *are* good." This would be an ongoing collection, twenty-five-plus years in the accumulating, of his personal "greatest records ever made" (in his view, all classical and jazz. One of my own choices, the Monkees's *Pisces, Aquarius, Capricorn & Jones, Ltd*, is notably absent). The middle floor houses the ones he actually plays on a more or less regular basis—again a collection high in snob appeal, though his taste in pop testifies that nobody's perfect. The sight of Beethoven and Sonny Rollins filed right next to Loggins &

Messina bears out the wonders of personal choice—though as he assures me, the Loggins & Messina album is really well recorded.

His selection is, in fact, far better than what you'd probably find at your local Tower Records. Maybe they'll have one copy of Miles Davis's fusion classic *Bitches Brew*, but he's got three—different pressings from different countries in different decades—all sitting side by side. The Japanese pressing from the '80s sounds fine, he tells me, but what you really want is the freshest pressing from the album's country of origin. That's just what I find next to the Japanese one: the original Columbia pressing of *Bitches Brew*, with the bolder type that the company used on record labels at that time, still bearing the original cover sticker ("Specially Priced 2-Record Set!") and its original price tag of $5.69. He has replaced the original paper inner sleeves with plastic-lined ones, so the record slides right out. I can't find a scratch or a sign of wear anywhere on it. No matter how many times it's been played in the past 30 years, this is a record that's never been taken lightly.

Why he's driven to acquire this stuff is a mystery, even to himself. "You know how collectors are," is his first response when pressed for an explanation. But, he does admit that it goes back to a girl, Marjorie, the cute librarian in Sioux City, Iowa, who first turned him on to classical music. Though he lost touch with her long ago, the fixation has remained. "Every man needs something to amuse him. It's an indulgence. I'm well off, and there are a lot of well-heeled people in the collecting biz. Besides, access to this stuff will all be over someday—it will all be collected. So we record collec-

tors are driven in a way that other collectors cannot be."
Having worked for a record label myself, I can see his point.
I've seen piles of albums that were no longer selling get sliced
down the middle and sent off to be used as landfill. My sym-
pathies went out to the collectors who might have unknow-
ingly driven right over the object of their search.

But the subject that gets him going is that of the vast,
silver-circle conspiracy of the industry to replace his beloved
vinyl with those cold, soulless CDs. In fact, the era that gave
us compact discs, namely the past twenty years, can be written off in his book as well. "Modern recording studios are
like intensive care units," he says, the epigrams rolling off his
tongue as if he'd been saving them for such an occasion. "Music is all about the groove, and you don't find grooves on a
CD. Give me the sound of old 78s over your tinkly LPs and
edgy CDs—and I hope you'll quote me on that," he declares.
To prove his point somewhat, he recalls a day at the studio
he used to run, when his usual group of cohorts was spinning
their vintage jazz vinyl. "Then this twenty-year-old kid came
in, carrying a bag of CDs," he recalls, a conspiratorial grin
lighting up his eyes. "And he says to me, 'Who told you
records are better? I should know what's best—I'm a junior
at MIT! I am studying this stuff!' " Johnson rolls his eyes and
rests his case: CDs must be bad if someone so unhip would
swear by them.

A number of industry insiders would agree with Johnson, if
not for the same reasons. Bob Irwin, for one, shares his target

audience's love for vinyl. "For me it goes back to when I was five years old and started returning any soda bottle I could get my hands on, to get enough change to buy a 45 or an LP. Later on, when I had a job, I remember hitting every record store in a thirty-mile radius, getting those three-for-a-buck LPs. Anything that I heard about when I was a kid, I'd try to get my hands on. Getting a record was a wonderful thing, and it wasn't just the music—it was the smell of it, the look of the inner sleeve. My CDs now live comfortably with my LPs. If we're having a dinner party I can crank up the one hundred-CD changer. But when friends are over, I like nothing better than running back and forth from the shelves to the turntable."

One of the most recent releases on Sundazed—a mono restoration of Bob Dylan's *Bringing It All Back Home*—is one that lives up to its title. The music itself can't bring any revelations by now. Sure, it's a classic, but it's nearly forty years old, and most of us are probably as sick of the songs, at this point, as Dylan is. But, if you're jaded enough to feel that way, you're also old enough to get a cheap thrill when you pull the reissue out of the cover and see that old, salmon-red Columbia label again. The vinyl even clings to the inner sleeve as you draw it out for the first time—something that never happens again once you play the disc and its virginity is lost.

The folks at Sundazed have done their homework, finding the vaults the original masters were locked in, locating the negatives of the cover photo, and pressing it all on virgin vinyl (as opposed to the cheaper, recycled stuff). At the end of the day, it's almost—but not quite—as good as the plain

old mono album that you could have bought at your neighborhood department store for three dollars the first time
around. "If you're lucky enough to have a 1-A pressing of
the album, it was a truly wonderful record," admits Sundazed
owner Irwin. "They had the ears of everybody from Bob on
down, listening and approving them, it was the way they
wanted the record to sound. If you have the literal first pressing, it would sound awesome. But as we move away from the
original lacquer, the experience gets lost."

Bill Inglot makes his living preserving that experience.
Working for Motown, Rhino, Atlantic, and many other labels, he's been entrusted with creating the CD masters for
some of the highest-regarded music of the vinyl era. His aesthetic is hard to pin down, but he's got a definite sense of
what sounds good. For certain records, including some '60s
soul classics, he's certain that the mono versions sound better
than the stereo ones, so he's done his bit to keep those in
circulation. Not everyone is convinced that the Supremes's
"Baby Love" sounds heavier in mono, but indeed it does.
The clarity and presence he's drawn out of the Ray Charles,
Aretha Franklin and Everly Brothers catalogs—and for that
matter, *Bo Donaldson & the Heywoods's Greatest Hits*, which
sounds far better than it even should—speaks for itself.

Simple as it seems, what he's confirmed is something that
every collector knows: those irrational, indefinable some-
things that define your listening experience are precisely
what it's all about. If you think vinyl is warmer and more seductive, then you're right. If you like CDs because they're
sharper (or at least, louder), then you're right, too. So much

for the definitive arguments that got presented when CDs started wiping vinyl off the map, that their sound was inherently superior, that those digital bits could hold more and better information.

That's not a claim to dismiss out of hand: listening to the new mastering that Inglot and Andrew Sandoval did of Elvis Costello's *This Year's Model*, I'm hearing a tambourine on the intro of "You Belong to Me" that was never there before—and I can finally hear the whole song with the ear-crushing volume I longed for when I was blasting the vinyl on my mid-'70s Magnavox stereo. However, a vinyl partisan would answer that the tambourine should have been mixed higher in the first place, that the vinyl album had more presence at any volume, and that I should have owned a better amplifier in the '70s. Before we put the sex metaphor out of its misery, let's just say that it's a simple matter of whatever turns you on.

"There are bad CDs out there," says Inglot. "And there are some I've been involved with that sound better than the original LP. That doesn't mean we're God, and it doesn't mean the originals were crap. It does mean that technology can serve as well as brutalize music. There are certain things that vinyl can do better because of its limitations, which makes it more of an emotional listening experience. The physical limitations of dragging a rock along a dirt road [ie, running a chip of diamond over a plastic field at 33 rpm] can forgive a multitude of issues about how the music is recorded. It kind of mushes things just right." And, he says, you can't evaluate either without considering the subjective factors, like the sentimental attachment to vinyl and the functionality of CDs. "When CDs came along, they freed us from our turntables. That doesn't mean turntables don't have their place, but so does all the information in the *World Book Encyclopedia*. And if you're going to the beach, which do you want to bring—that or a trashy Harold Robbins novel?"

So take note: here's someone whose career has risen with the CD, who knows how many knobs and dials, how much smoke and mirrors it takes to turn out a compact disc, and he's willing not only to admit that he listens to vinyl at home, but to compare the hot medium to trashy novels and safe sex. As for the question of whether CDs sound better than vinyl, the answer is: sometimes they do and sometimes they don't. There are just too many variables—how well the master tape has held up, whether the remastering engineer can get inside the original engineer's head—to give either medium the objective upper hand.

Exactly what Inglot and his collaborators do in the studio has changed over the years. When CDs were young, he was into recreating exactly what was done in the studio twenty or thirty years earlier, which meant he went back to the original, unmixed, multitrack tapes that were spun in the studio and mixed them from scratch, trying to recreate exactly what the original producer had done, only allowing for the additional frequency response you'd get on a CD. One of my favorite results was "Walk Away Renee" by the Left Banke. It was also one of Inglot's more heroic moments. While reconstructing the track, he and Sandoval figured out that the lead vocal had, in fact, been performed twice, and that the original producer had cut and pasted from the two vocals, line by line. Such ventures gave him the power, to not quite change history, but to tweak it a little bit. He could decide that the strings in "Walk Away Renee" needed to be sharper, or to undo a particularly lame stereo mix (the original one for the Monkees's "Pleasant Valley Sunday" was limp as it gets).

"Some people think I'm the devil," he admits. "Just try going to a search engine and typing in 'Bill Inglot sucks.' " I did, and could, in fact, find only three people who thought he sucked – all steamed over his decision to put mono mixes on a '60s soul box. But he admits he's less inclined to leave his own fingerprints on a record. "When I was younger and more immature, I probably wanted to remix the world, and that's not a place that I really want to go anymore. A lot of times you get something that might be better, but it's not quite the same. Even if it's 1965 and you're going in to mix 'Mr. Tambourine Man' the day after it was recorded, something's still changed since then." For example, he recently restored some tracks by one of the trippiest '60s bands, the Electric Prunes. When it came to that band's greatest hit, whatever happened in the studio circa 1967—wild inspiration, really good acid, or dumb luck—proved impossible to figure out, much less duplicate. "You put up the multitracks of 'I Had Too Much to Dream Last Night'—now that's a four-track recording, it shouldn't be brain surgery. But we could get no concept of how they got from point A to point B. You could spend years on it, and it's still not gonna be right. Like most things people do, they didn't put a lot of thought into it. It could be serendipity, or it could be dust in the console." He let the original mix stand.

His own feelings about vinyl are a bit conflicted, disdaining a preoccupation that he admits to sharing. "Vinyl is something we grew up with. You started with singles, and those were like training wheels, then you moved up to albums. If you skip down a generation or two, that feeling will probably vanish. As it is, I think nothing of forking out a couple hundred bucks for a rare LP, but I have a hard time paying more than retail for a rare CD. The real emotional experience is the music, but the vinyl is an emotional experience as well, there are very realistic, and somewhat subjective, rationales for it being a better medium. But when you get down to it, who cares? The patient has washed up on the beach here, and it's not coming back. You can walk around thinking vinyl is better, but it's like wanting your girlfriend from high school who is now married with three kids. You can only have a piece of your past for so long."

Most vinyl lovers would agree that the format harks back to the past, but not everyone thinks there's anything necessarily wrong with that, says Roger Manning. "I don't necessarily advocate living in the past, but there's a reason we do that—we're not getting enough stimulus from what's going on currently. People tend to forget what it was like to put on your headphones and go on a journey." Manning has lately worked with a handful of very modern artists—playing keyboards for Beck and doing remixes for the French electronic band Air—and his love for vinyl has come into play there. "You go back to the recording equipment that was in vogue during the '70s, and the low-fi element of the scratched vinyl, and there's good reason why that sound holds up in a club. It's funny that because a lot of old jazz is being sampled now, you are finding a lot of young kids, a lot of scenesters and clubgoers, who are getting praise, laurels and dates with women because they listen to people like Herbie Hancock. In my day, listening to Herbie Hancock would have gotten you beaten up."

Surprisingly enough, the most outspoken CD proponent I found was the hip-hop DJ Lucas MacFadden, a/k/a Cut Chemist, whose life and work are closely tied to vinyl. As a member of the underground hip-hop crew Jurassic 5, he's found new angles for the use of scratches and samples as a field for rapping. Performing solo and in collaboration with DJ Shadow, he's pioneered the turntable as an improvisational instrument in its own right. And he allows that love for vintage vinyl was one thing that initially drew him into the DJ world.

Like many in the hip-hop community, Chemist traces his own roots back to J.B.—but in his case that means James Bond, not James Brown. It was the style of those Bond soundtrack covers, with the pretty girls and the sleek '60s lettering, that drew him in as a kid. "I didn't give two shits about the music, but I started with *From Russia With Love* and wound up collecting them all. Those real seductive covers—everything had its own theme; I just kept going after them. That was my first real impulse, 'I want to collect this, I want to have all of them.' Even if I didn't like the music,

they were still better than baseball cards because they at least
had the music on them. They were something functional. I
was never a big reader, never into sports, so my function of
choice was getting those records. I think I stopped with
Moonraker, because I was finally getting older and it was like,
'Hold on, what am I doing?' "

By then the other J.B. had also come into play, thanks to
a compilation album that bent a lot of ears in the '80s. "The
album, *In the Jungle Groove*—I heard that beat and I went out
to find it. It was that one, 'Little Miss Lover' by Jimi Hendrix,
and 'Take Me to the Mardi Gras' by Bob James, those were
all on my first break tape. Doing the first tape was important,
because I'd wanted to be Mr. DJ ever since I was eight years
old and buying all those K-Tel compilation records."

Today Chemist characterizes his collection as "Not many—
just somewhere between ten and twenty thousand [a figure
that few non-collectors would call "not many"]—but at least
they're all good." And his approach to record-buying isn't
that different from what it was in the Bond days. "I don't buy
them to listen to, so much as I do because I like to look at
'em. I buy things for my collection when they have historical
significance for me. I like buying funk 45s, old soul albums.
I buy them to file, really. What I like to buy are things that
I've never seen before, and there's still tons of rap releases I
haven't seen. Those are hip, so it's important to have those
collected."

His instincts as a DJ are considerably different, treating a
record as a guitarist might think of a new set of strings. "You
just look for textures, and that could be anything, it could be

a guitar stab. Drums are always the first thing you look for, and you go on from there. Vinyl sounds different, whether it's a one hundred and fifty-gram record or one of those thin, old flexible ones. There's different degrees of natural compression in there. I try to play different kinds of music next to each other, to show how they all relate, whether it's a rock record or a drum-and-bass record. The manipulation of those sounds is important and that's what hip-hop is about: taking something that exists and reinventing it. Scratching is like talking and the more music you have at your disposal, the more you can say. You want to talk, you want to be as articulate as you can be."

That language inevitably comes down to his vinyl. "DJs are finding new ways to cope with digital technology, there are ways you can use MIDI and computer files to simulate a vinyl scratch. But when I see a DJ I want to see him pick up the needle and put it down on the vinyl—that's half of what it is to be a DJ giving a performance. The way he manipulates the vinyl is a big part of the appeal."

All of which would naturally lead to a speech about the superiority of vinyl, but for Chemist it's quite the opposite. "We're a digital generation, my friend, let's face up to it. It's true, there are certain tonalities of vinyl that digital technology can't produce, but we're getting away from it. Sure, I love records because I experienced the record in its heyday, there's the smell of the paper and the pictures are bigger, with liner notes that you can read. But I think that if you take a ten-year-old kid that's never seen a record before, that kid will like the CD more. It's smaller and the kid will think it looks cooler. Every generation has its medium for listening to music. For our parents' generation it was vinyl. For us it's CDs, and for the next it will probably be MP3s. In order for our society to evolve to where it has to go, we need to let go of the past, and vinyl is part of the past."

Chapter Five

ON THE ROAD I:
RELICS IN TEXAS

*C**ut Chemist* and Bill Inglot may come from different corners of the music world, but both seem to agree that vinyl represents a part of the past that you can't return to. That's the bad news. The good news is that you can still have a piece of somebody else's past. For instance, I don't even know who used to own the copy of Buck Owens's *Minute Masters* that I found in a record convention in Austin, Texas, but I can assure them that it's in good hands.

Some collectors don't even go to record conventions, pointing out that most of the dealers get to pick each other's prizes before the everyday folks even show up. But a record convention is one of the few occasions that will bring collectors out to meet each other, or at least to walk around in the same room at the same time. Most major cities have them at least once a year, the Austin event (along with the one radio station WFMU sponsors seasonally in New York) being best known. Appropriately, the New York show crams a lot of material into a smallish space, while the one in Texas is distinguished by its sprawl—the convention center looks like a round airplane hangar. Some of the attendees are clearly high-rollers, dressed in flashy cowboy hats and shades, with their doubtlessly valuable, 12-inch square parcels tucked under their arms and on their shoulders. Tourists are here too, out-of-towners trying to grab some of the city's musical history via an old concert poster or a piece of vintage country vinyl. The dabblers get turned away quickly. Go to one of the dealers hoping to unload the REO Speedwagon and Styx albums you collected in high school (current resale value: roughly thirty-three cents, aesthetic value: something similar) and you'll get laughed at. Of course, if you go in hoping to buy that same record, they'll probably dig up a copy to sell you for a few bucks. If you've spent any time hunting vinyl, a thrill of imminent consummation hits when you walk in the door.

Despite the number of collectors here, it's not that diverse a crowd. Men hovering at middle-age predominate, and their dress and attitude reflect a music-chasing lifestyle. The long hair, leather jackets and band T-shirts all show a sense of style cribbed from '60s and '70s music magazines. Many of the younger attendees are scraggly metalheads—apparently,

Led Zeppelin cultism knows no age barriers. Nobody stands out more than the couple of women with modern fashion sense, like the purple-haired punk girl who browses the old Stranglers badges at a new-wave booth. Every corner here has a different area of specialty, all giving a glimpse into a different musical world. One sells nothing but local concert posters, which represent a capsule version of this city's musical history. Browse through dozens of mini-posters advertising Willie Nelson and Jerry Jeff Walker appearances, mixed with those druggy dancing-frog cartoons beloved in the hippie era, and you can get a sense of what you missed by being born a few years too late. Who'd have thought that the artsy English band Gentle Giant once played at the down-home Armadillo World Headquarters, even prompting some long forgotten patron to scribble "this was cool" in the margin of the poster?

A few of these corridors are pure punk. Ironically enough, those profane T-shirts ("Fuck Art, Let's Dance") and Sex Pistols 45s with their defaced photos of the Queen, which spat in the face of propriety in 1977, are well-treasured collector's items today. Artifacts from the '60s are worth even more. Most of the kids who owned Monkees trading cards or Beatles action figures didn't take very good care of them, that's why a well-preserved one will fetch hundreds of dollars. Even bubblegum music has gained some retrospective value, since record collecting is as much about snapping up pieces of an era as it is about accumulating music. Teen magazines with Bobby Sherman's face on the cover? Bound to bring back a good memory for somebody. Partridge Family lunchboxes from 1970? Well, the era was cool even if the Partridges weren't.

Some booths have nothing but old jukebox singles. In the '50s and '60s, when the 45 was king, every soda shop and truckstop had a jukebox, and somebody remembered to stash away the records that finished their run to make way for the newest hit. Still others deal in fetish items like oddly-shaped discs, picture discs and colored vinyl, which enjoyed a brief vogue in the late '70s. Before the CD came along, record labels had to think of something to make people re-purchase albums they already had, and a copy of *Sgt. Pepper* with the big drum pressed into the vinyl did the trick. Not every booth is fully organized, some are a random jumble of radio-station promotional discs from the past two decades, some gems and some worthless, a collection that spilled out of a closet. But this is partly about the thrill of the hunt, and turning up that elusive find is that much sweeter if you uncover it behind a hill of crap.

One booth specializes in country rarities, and there I make my find: *Minute Masters*, a Buck Owens album that was produced in 1968, just for record-store play, on which twenty of Buck's hits were edited down to concise sixty-second versions to fit a shopper's limited attention span. No doubt that this record has been through the wars. Owens smiles from a black-and-white photo on the cover, and sometime between 1968 and now, someone decided to color in the singer's lips with a red magic marker. Another batch of markings was scribbled directly on the vinyl, to X out one of the songs—

evidently a tune called "Cajun Fiddle" was a real turnoff for the customers. For me it's not just 30 minutes of music, but a window into a different time and place. Maybe this record was played at a department store in the rural part of the state, with a soda fountain in the corner and the familiar country hits playing on a busy Saturday afternoon. The red squiggles can probably be washed off later, meanwhile they've driven the disc's value down to a very affordable ten dollars—not a bad price for an artifact. How many listeners ever get to savor nearly two dozen Buck Owens hits in twenty minutes flat? The knowledge that this was the only copy of this disc I'd ever see added to the appeal. And if whoever ran that store didn't want to hear "Cajun Fiddle"—a pretty decent instrumental, as it turns out—I'm more than glad to annoy my neighbors with it now.

Huddled in one corner are a trio of collectors who've found their personal Holy Grail, and an unlikely one it is. It's a perfect collector's record, in part because there's no explanation for it, it's a musical force of nature. The singer is French pop star Michel Polnareff, most of whose records were hits with the suave romantics at home. Not this one, however. "Time Will Tell" was a failed attempt to crack the mid-'60s American market, complete with a picture sleeve showing the singer in a sensitive pose, and displaying the phonetic pronunciation of his name. But the song is anything but sensitive—it's an early punk rock number, the singer's attempt to plug into the American garage trend that came about when '6os kids tried to sound like the Beatles and Stones, and failed gloriously. The result was a million variations on "Louie Louie" tumbling out of suburban garages, and "Time Will Tell" was yet another, with the requisite three chords and a primal fuzz-guitar sound. Hearing a French crooner tackle this number is ridiculous, but it's also great. It's got that hormone-driven, out-of-control quality you can find in the best '6os punk records. That the singer is clearly struggling with his English only adds to the effect. Most of the great '6os garage records were made by Jagger-obsessed American kids faking British accents, so a French guy faking an American accent ("you say that you're my leetle ger-ul") doesn't sound all that different.

In a booth that specializes in '6os singles and memorabilia, three scraggly-haired guys in their mid-to-late thirties are huddled around a record player, savoring the moment. You'd think that a valuable record would have to be handled with care and played on a top-of-the-line stereo, but they're committing the apparent sin of playing it on a mono phonograph (it doesn't even earn the highfalutin' word "turntable") made of bright red plastic with white volume and tone knobs. The machine must be at least as old as the record, and it's the kind of heavy-tracking monster that wears away the vintage grooves with every play. But a record like this was made for the thrill of the moment, and these have to be the best circumstances for listening. The crappy player makes the song sound like it would have sounded on AM radio, it renders the production more unearthly and makes the fuzz guitar sound even fuzzier. So the three huddled listeners are getting close to the essence, getting to hear the song in its natural element. One of them, a shaggy blonde who plays local clubs with his own band, resolves to learn the tune and maybe pass it off as an original. No problem if somebody recognizes it, because digging up a song like this is nearly as cool as writing one. Conversation hushes as the record reaches its peak—a wild falsetto bridge that finds Polnareff sounding like a street-corner doo-wopper from Mars. At this the dealer nods his head sagely: "It just never stops being good."

*S*ometimes *it* all comes down to that girl in the record store. If you happened to be a pre-teen guy in the mid-'6os, the record store was an exciting enough place to start—all those colors, all those LPs, all that exotic music, the possibility that your fave band might have released something since you last visited. If you also happen to have a crush on the girl behind the counter, you can get hooked for life. Peter Buck is living proof.

"I think her name was Susan," recalls the lanky guitarist, now well-known as one-third of R.E.M. "It was at a little proto-mall in California, a little square of shops with a record store in it. She was the older woman that I had a crush on, though she was probably all of twenty years old. She had go-

go boots, the whole nine yards. And she's always telling me, 'You don't want to buy that Tom Jones record. You want to buy something cooler, like this Rolling Stones record, or this Eric Burdon & the Animals record.' It was very influential to me that you tied these two things together—that kind of inchoate sexual urge, and buying records. I believe Freud says that there's a sexual component to collecting—but not having read Freud, I'm either totally naïve or I'm just a huge pervert."

That girl in the store figures in many a collector's history, and she usually serves to sexualize an obsession that was already brewing. That was definitely the case with Buck. "I was already obsessed. Everyone else was more into baseball, which I liked okay. But my dad had a homebuilt Heathkit stereo, and I could not keep my hands off it. My dad happened to like Ray Charles, that was nice. My mom liked Burl Ives, and I think I'm scarred for life because of that. They finally had to buy me a little close-and-play turntable because I couldn't leave theirs alone, and that was just in time for the Beatles. I still have the first record I bought—'A Hard Day's Night' in the original picture sleeve, which I cut in half and tacked to the wall everywhere I've lived. I can afford to buy a pristine mint copy now, but I want the worn-to-shit single in the plastic bag. That's where I come from."

Susan's whereabouts are lost to history, but record stores remain Buck's first love. There's a reason he gets along so well with rock critics and other music-heads, they recognize him as part of the same breed. It's a popular part of R.E.M. mythology that Buck was working at a record store—Wuxtry

Records in Athens, Georgia, still one of the town's hotspots for imports and indie-rock releases—when the band was formed. (Stuffed with used vinyl and lined with gig flyers, Wuxtry still looks like a collector's living room after a tornado hit, and that's a good thing.) After R.E.M. had their first taste of nationwide success, at the point when most rock stars think of buying a house in the Bahamas, Buck wound up working at Wuxtry again. "I think it was 1986, which was the first year we didn't tour 350 days a year. My old boss said to me, 'Don't you ever miss working?' and he was right. I missed that whole process of checking in, doing the count and having the records there. So I worked there every Monday for maybe four months. I didn't take any money because I didn't want to deal with that, but we added it up and I had enough credit to get the import Muddy Waters box. So I was happy, except that the liner notes were in Japanese."

Like many collectors, Buck never shook his childhood memories of the record store as a magical place. "I had the quintessentially great record store experience," he recalls. "I was living in Montrose, California, just north of Glendale. There was one hip record store out there where everyone had hair down to their shoulders, the guys had beards, the chicks looked like chicks look now. I was thirteen, I walked in there and said 'I'd do anything to work here.' Finally they said, 'Okay, you can sweep up once or twice a week, and we'll give you discounts on records.' Which, knowing what I know about retail now, means that they had me working for free for a whole year. I figured they were probably cheating me a little bit, but I got treated like an adult by these older people, these guys with huge beards. They'd tell me things like, 'You've gotta get out of here because I'm going to smoke some pot.' And I'm like, 'Wow, man! I heard about that! Can I smoke some pot, too?' And they said, 'No, you've got to go out back.' So I went back and swept the floor while they smoked the herb."

So the young Buck struck out on the sex and drugs, but at least he got the rock 'n' roll. "Yeah, I got great records. That first James Taylor record [*Sweet Baby James*] that wasn't on Apple? Got it the day it came out. The first Black Sabbath album? Got it the day it came out. Then I moved to Georgia and fell in with the guy who ran the record store there—he was 280 pounds, with a beard and hair down to his waist. Totally stoned all the time. But he liked me, and I was fourteen. He'd call me up and say something like [in conspiratorial whisper] 'Hey, that new Stones album, *Exile on Main Street*, it's coming out tonight.' He'd call my house and I'd have to hitchhike fifteen miles to get to the store. And hitchhiking in Georgia, if it's 1972 and you have hair down to your shoulders? Totally fucked. A bad, bad experience. You were either getting beat up, or having things thrown at you, or getting propositioned by people you didn't want to get propositioned by. But I'd hitchhike in, get the record and then hitchhike back out."

There's a number of reference points Buck shares with anyone who became a vinyl junkie in the '70s. Even something as commonplace as the Velvet Underground's first album—which you can now get in at least three different CD formats—was officially out of print in the late '70s, just when a host of punk bands were insisting that you go out and find yourself one. "That's why I started collecting, because I come from an era where everything was out of print. You couldn't get any John Coltrane. Miles Davis's *On the Corner* went out of print the year after it came out. Even *Pet Sounds* [the Beach Boys album that's both a legit masterpiece and a critical sacred cow] was hard to find. Today you can sit down on Amazon and get everything delivered to your house. But my collecting impulse came from knowing that the airwaves were full of England Dan & John Ford Coley, things I didn't want to hear. And what were the record stores floating? Bullshit. There was good music out there, but you found a lot of it used or remaindered. I found the Skip Spence album *Oar* for 29 cents in a bargain bin in Roswell, Georgia. It's beat to shit, but I still have the same copy."

In his years behind record-store counters, he had no qualms about pushing the right records on people. In fact, there's probably more than a few Georgians who had their tastes warped for life when they went down to buy some current hit, and Buck sent them out with a Velvet Underground album instead. "I was the best retail salesman you've seen in your entire life. I couldn't sell cars or tin huts or anything, but as far as records go, I was always excited. They always did more business during my shifts, because I was so excited about the records. I wound up working at Doo Dah Records in Atlanta—a pretty straight little store, but me and one of the other guys who worked there ordered all these English imports."

Launching into his record-store rap, Buck shows a bravado

that he sometimes softens in R.E.M. interviews, where he maintains a degree of modesty. "I still think that if I ran retail, it would be my world. I'd have no trouble getting into it. Back in 1977, we had all these thirteen-year-olds coming into the store. They'd ask me for a Judas Priest record and I'd say, 'Man, if you like Judas Priest, I'll tell you what you'll really like: The Ramones. They're really cool, and I think they're better for someone your age. I think you should buy the second Ramones record, as opposed to the eighth Judas Priest record.' Or they'd ask for Black Sabbath and I'd say, 'You like them? Okay, they're really great. But you know what—they broke up last year [or at least, they'd just lost Ozzy Osbourne]. So that's an old record. Why don't you buy a new one, like Cheap Trick's *In Color?*' There's a whole generation of kids in Atlanta that grew up with me forcing them to buy records. And I still run into those kids, except that they're 39 now."

In other words, he wound up doing for those Atlanta kids what Susan did for him, steering them away from the unhip items. "Yeah, but I doubt that any of those young kids wanted to have sex with me."

Despite his status as a musician, Buck is still very much a collector—and one sure giveaway is his faint protests to the contrary. "It's way bigger than my house can hold, unfortunately. Probably ten thousand vinyl albums, eight to ten thousand singles, and the CDs, I don't even want to talk about.

Okay, I have a huge collection of records. But at least they're things I play, I don't buy them to look at them." You mean you have time to play all twenty-odd thousand? "Okay, there's a little sickness in there. I don't think my wife understood the depth of my obsession until we got a house together. I've got books, too, maybe ten to fifteen thousand of those, and she said we couldn't possibly bring those along. But you know what? To me it's not a house unless I can have my books and records in it. So we decided we didn't really eat in that much, so the dining room became the record room—and then the toy room, when our two kids were born. A toy room with fourteen feet of records in it. We wound up building a dining room on the other end of the house, and now that's become the second book and record room instead."

In other words, he reached critical mass long ago. "Considering that I still buy them every day, definitely. If I allotted a forty-hour week, eight hours a day, and played records the whole time, I could never finish them all. But I really tried one time. I'd pull out things I hadn't played for twenty years, put 'em on and play at least one side, then make sure they were filed back correctly. And I barely made a dent. It's not often that people come over to my house. But when they do I wind up saying, 'You gotta hear this.' It's usually something like the Louie & the Lovers record—have you heard that one?" I admit being stumped. "Now that's a motherfucker record. Produced by [Texas rock legend] Doug Sahm. It sounds like a Chicano Creedence from 1967. I read about it in *Rolling Stone* and bought it for 19 cents, and I still pull it out and play it. And I hope it's still under 'L' when I look for it."

What about people who obsessively collect R.E.M. records? "Hey, they made a pretty good choice. I see those people all the time and it blows my mind, because I'm usually so anal about that kind of thing—I know every Elvis Costello B-side, but I don't know anything about my own. I don't remember which singles came from which record, and I can't necessarily remember what songs are on what albums. They come to have me sign things and I'm like, 'What the hell is this? I don't even remember making this record.' And I think that's great. When you make a record there's no way you can appreciate it anyway, other than appreciating its faults. So for me, I listen to R.E.M. and I'm thinking, it could have been so much better—and it really could have been. But I accept the fact that it's also finished, it's gone. Otherwise we'd still be working on *Murmur* [their full-length debut from two decades earlier]."

Being a well-known rocker does have its drawbacks, however. It makes it harder to tastefully unload the records you don't want—especially when a band you didn't like in the '70s comes back to haunt you. "I have boxes in the basement that I can't even look at. I get a lot in the mail now, which is something you think is ideal when you're younger. But you wouldn't believe how much you just don't want to hear, and I can't sell it because that would look really cheesy. So let me know if there's anyone that wants the first four Judas

Priest albums with bonus tracks—because I can't sell them, and I don't want them in my house."

Soon after our interview, Buck is selling records again. He's on a package tour with his instrumental band Tuatara, and this tour is so democratic that whoever's not onstage takes a turn selling merchandise. I spot him putting in his shift, at a booth to the side of the stage where he's arranged the sale CDs—by the musicians playing that night in various combinations—along the top of a cocktail table. He presses a CD into my hands. "Here's a Minus Five album you haven't heard," he notes, indicating a rarities disc by another of his non-R.E.M. bands. "Its pretty rare, you can't buy it in stores. And you know what? Since it's so hard to find, it's perfect for someone who's writing a book about record collectors. I'll let you have it for ten bucks."

Damn, the guy really is good. I tuck the disc in my pocket and make a mental note to hunt down Louie & the Lovers next time around.

Chapter Seven
ROBERT CRUMB: "COLLECTING IS CREEPY"

*Y*ou collect '60s psychedelic records?" asks an incredulous Robert Crumb as if I'd just let on that I had a house full of severed heads. "I hate that music. I think it's one of the worst kinds of music that there ever was."

Yes, this is the same R. Crumb who practically invented underground comics, who helped put the phrase 'Keep on truckin'' into the vernacular with a cartoon that hit college walls everywhere, and whose album cover for Big Brother & the Holding Company's *Cheap Thrills* was something of a psychedelic-era icon. More to the point, it's the same R. Crumb who's been collecting prewar 78s for the past three decades, and is seldom known to listen to anything else. His roomful of shellac was proudly displayed in the biopic *Crumb*, directed by his friend and fellow enthusiast Terry Zwigoff. Crumb himself has recorded as the leader of the revival band Cheap Suit Serenaders, and many of his cartoons have referred to the spirit and the personalities of early jazz and blues.

"Collecting is creepy," Crumb tells me with some degree of pride. "Record collectors put each other down for their various fixations. Everybody is convinced that his way of collecting is superior. They look down on casual collectors, who are just accumulators—the kind who'll just pick up anything and let it pile up. A true collector is more of a connoisseur, and that's the good thing about collecting. It creates a connoisseurship to sort out what's worthwhile in the culture and what isn't. Wealthy art collectors in this country have sorted out who the great artists are. If you're collecting a lot of objects of one particular kind, you develop a very acute sense of discrimination."

This, of course, doesn't keep them from being creepy. "You saw the scene in Terry Zwigoff's movie *Ghost World*— that about says it all," he says—referring to the party scene where a bunch of geeky male collectors fondle each other's collections while the two hip women in the room roll their eyes. "I know all those guys. Any of the younger guys who get into 78 collecting are quirky and oddball types, pretty maladjusted people. They're not into hanging around in bars and picking up chicks or nothing. If they have a girlfriend at all it's amazing. And the older collectors I know, a lot of them just have their little room down in the basement where they go and listen. They don't share it with anyone, and their wives don't know anything about it. So when they die, the vultures start descending."

Crumb's collection is almost entirely shellac. He keeps vinyl and CDs around only when he wants a song he can't get in the original format. "78 collectors have almost nothing to do with LP or 45 collectors; prewar collectors have nothing to do with postwar collectors. They don't avoid each other, but they bully and pick on each other. That's the problem, it's lonely collecting records. You can share it, but there's a vicious undercurrent there, the only person you can ever impress with that rare record you just got is another collector who's looking for the same record. And the average person, I can show them the rarest record in the collection and they'll say, 'Yeah? So what?' "

This in fact happened to him in the '70s, when a publisher demonstrated his eternal uncoolness. "I did try to share it with the world, I did comic stories about old musicians because I thought it was far superior to anything being done currently. In this case, I had done a comic story about Charley Patton, one of the great fathers of the blues, and the guy who published it was over at my house. So I took out one of my favorite 78s, Charley Patton's 'Down the Dirt Road,' and I put it on. So I'm sitting there, having this great experience listening to this record, and he's sitting there quietly, patiently. And after I took it off, he looks at me and says, 'So, what did you like about that?' " Crumb laughs. "I mean, he wasn't trying to be insulting, just curious, but what can you say to that? So I don't try to convert people anymore."

But the saddest, most tragic aspect of collecting, as he admits, is that it won't get you any action. "Picking up chicks? Forget it! It never gets them hot, they don't give a shit about collectors. I wouldn't say that collectors are antisocial—that would imply that they want to do something harmful to society—but it's not very sociable either. Very self-obsessed, kind of asocial. That's why the world looks down on collectors, it takes a certain kind of personality. There is nothing sexy or glamorous about it. Women aren't attracted to people because they collect. You can go up to them and say, 'I'm an outlaw bandit' and they'll like that. But if you say, 'I'm a collector'—no chance."

His collection may be the stuff of legend, but here's the surprise: it numbers only about four thousand 78s. By that standard, he's pretty un-creepy for a collector: eight thousand songs is a reasonable amount to absorb in one lifetime, a small enough collection to keep in one room (Crumb stores his in some shelving he got for forty bucks in California). Having purged his collection a few times, and moved it across the Atlantic Ocean when he relocated to the south of France, he made the non-anal move of only holding onto the ones he expected to play on a regular basis. "I don't like to have music on as background, or to listen while I work. That's what I like about 78s, they force you to get up every three minutes and decide what you want to listen to again. It keeps you focused."

And unlike the folks he's just described, he can indeed sustain a relationship. "My wife had never heard any of this music, she was in her early 20s when we met. But she started hanging around my little cabin in the country. I played her some records and she immediately liked them. Thank God she doesn't collect psychedelic music from the '60s! I know people who've had to deal with worse problems. Terry Zwigoff had a girlfriend who listened to what he called 'old hippie lady music'—Jackson Browne, Joni Mitchell. It became a real bone of contention between them and it drove him crazy that the music irritated him so much. She dragged him to a Bob Dylan concert and the audience was so worshipful of Bob Dylan. At one point they all stood up, and they're clapping in unison, and he was the only one in the audience who refused to stand up."

Crumb's own aesthetic was formed at an early age. As a teenager in Delaware, he had a small epiphany at a farmer's market. "I had a natural bent to collecting: before it was records it was comic books, trading cards, all kinds of things. When I was in my early teens I started yearning to hear older music. I already knew I liked it more than what I was hearing on the radio. One day, out of curiosity, I was in this second-hand store, they had a lot of old books and things, and I started thinking, 'I wonder if they have any of this old music that I've been trying to find?' Lo and behold, they did and that was a real defining moment for me. My first one was 'Happy Days and Lonely Nights,' a Victor 78 by Charlie Fry. And I remember how great it felt to take that record home."

Locating prize 78s during the mid-'60s was an inexact science. You simply went into the black neighborhoods and knocked on peoples' doors, hoping that they had stockpiled some 78s a few decades ago and that they might be willing to part with them. "I didn't have the resources to make a lot of big trips, but people were doing that. A lot of guys in those days, they would go through the South canvassing for records, going door to door. Richard Nevins [founder of the folk label Shanachie] did that, and John Fahey [the late experimental guitarist] did it. The depression in the '30s killed a lot of the record business, since the records weren't selling in great numbers. So there'd be people holding onto them, and there's always fanatical collectors trying to find those people. It took a lot of detective work—finding someone who'd say, 'Oh yeah, so-and-so down the street has a lot of records in his barn.'

"You got great records that way, but it was a huge amount of work. And it was dangerous in the South; if you went into the black neighborhoods, the cops would bust you. A white guy knocking on peoples' doors—they didn't like that. I started going into the Salvation Army, and then to the black sections of town, where the houses would have old Victrolas in them. They'd have records stashed behind the couch or in the closet. I'd give them ten or twenty-five cents, and usually they'd accept that. There was this one lady, though, she started yelling at me—'You think I'm an ignorant old colored woman? I know that record is worth more than that! Don't you go pulling that smart stuff on me, boy!' And she was right, I would have given her more money, but I didn't have it. She had a record I really wanted. It took me twenty-five years to find another copy."

Living in the Bay Area at the height of the psychedelic explosion, Crumb let those records and that movement pass by. Why go after those records when you can find something as exotic as releases on the Flexo label—a short-lived San Francisco outfit that made 78s that actually bent? "Nobody knows what they're made of, because they kept the formula a secret. It was a small company in the '20s and '30s who actually made nonbreakable, flexible records, and they've held up pretty well over the years. And there's some really excellent music on them—San Francisco jazz and dance bands who have only been on Flexo. Over the years I lived out there, I only ever found two or three of them. Terry beat me on that one: he looked in the phone book and found that one of the bandleaders was still alive. And somehow I never thought of using the phone book—that shows that I don't have that kind of resourceful, hustling mind."

And that's enough to prove Crumb's point: only someone with a slightly twisted mind would, at this very moment, be getting excited at the idea of a 78 that bends. "Any collecting involves a bit of fetishism, it just depends on which one you've gotten fixated on at some point in your life. Once that's in place, very few collectors I know have ever expanded beyond that first fixation. For me, the 78 is a special talisman in itself, it has an aura that's different from that of a CD or an LP. It's as close as you can get to the original source of what the music was recorded on—even with the scratching and the surface noise, there is an aura. Because somebody before you originally bought that 78, it was sitting in the shop at some point soon after the music was recorded. Somebody of that era bought it and listened to it, and that record carries that aura from whoever else had handled and appreciated that object."

Fetishism does have its rewards. "When I was younger I was more obsessed," he admits. "But I've gotten most of the ones I really yearned for when I was young, my dream records—the ones you could only imagine ever finding. Even now, I'll pull my copy of 'What's That Tastes Like Gravy?' by the King Davis Jug Band out of my collection and feel amazed that I actually own it."

Chapter Eight

45 R P M

ON THE ROAD 2:
SOUL HEART TRANSPLANT

*R*ecord collector
John Tefteller
gets a phone call one afternoon, from a guy who saw his
name on the internet. "I know you collect blues records,"
says the guy, "and I just picked up a stack of them at a thrift
shop in Nashville." Having fielded hundreds of calls like this,
Tefteller takes it with a grain of salt, and asks the guy to read
off the titles. The first few are nothing special, but then come
the magic words: "This one's on the Paramount label, and
it's by someone named Blind Joe Reynolds."

Based in Grants Pass, Oregon, John Tefteller has received
the ultimate compliment. Even Robert Crumb thinks he's
truly obsessed. Tefteller claims a six-figure income from deal-
ing rare records and has paid as much as eleven thousand

dollars for prize finds. At forty-three, he's relatively young to be harboring a fetish for shellac records that were made three decades before he was born. But having a minority taste is one advantage he enjoys. Another is his smooth-talking manner, with a voice that could easily belong to a seasoned DJ. An outgoing personality is always an asset, when you're trying to get folks in their 70s to look through stacks of records that they stashed in their attic a couple generations ago.

Having devoted much of his life to tracking down rare blues 78s, Tefteller knew from that phone call that he'd just hit paydirt. What the guy had wasn't even Reynolds's famous record—"Outside Woman Blues," a minor classic that Eric Clapton covered with Cream—but the followup, "Cold Woman Blues." Collectors knew that this one existed, since there are master lists of Paramount releases, but nobody until now had ever found a copy—it was never reissued or transferred to CD, so the record was lost to history. Assuming the guy didn't do anything stupid, the world's supply of vintage, late-'20s blues had just been increased by two songs.

"Great," says Tefteller, "Just tell me where the record is." "Oh," says the guy, "I tracked down a disc jockey in Washington, D.C., who wanted to hear it. So I mailed it to him." Now take into account everything you know about shellac records, figure in anything you know about the U.S. Post Office, and sure enough, the guy did something stupid.

"My heart sank. Now we know this record exists, and we know that we're never going to hear it." Miraculously enough, the record made it to D.C. in one piece. Tefteller not only had to head to D.C. to retrieve it, he also had to outbid the DJ who wanted to buy it himself. One road trip, much negotiating and a few thousand dollars later, he made the score.

This is where record detecting moves into the big leagues, taking on an element of intrigue that garden-variety collectors don't have to deal with. When I've scrounged through record bins, I was strictly in amateur class. For one thing I was in record stores, and well-known ones that tourists go to—bad idea, considering the number of music fans who'd been there before me. For another, I was in places like Memphis and New Orleans—great music towns, but ones whose supply of original vinyl has been picked clean over the past four decades. I came away with a few treasures, but any dabbler who's seen an Elvis movie or *The Big Easy* could have gotten there before me.

Can't say it wasn't fun, however. I've spent the last few years having a long-distance love affair with New Orleans music, and I've long made it past the obvious hits and gone in search of the rarities—which I've learned are often better than the songs everybody knows. For instance, a chestnut like the Meters's "Hey Pocky Way" may be great, but you've really got to hear the Party Boys's "We Got a Party"—a demented, audio-verite anthem to excess apparently recorded by a bunch of drunks when the studio crew wasn't looking. (After bragging that they got the party, the women and the whiskey, they drop this timeless chorus: "I can't hardly stand up/ Won't somebody help me?") Hearing the record, you're invited to picture the celebration that must have been going on inside that studio. I like to figure that they left the window open so people on the street could get into it. (According to legend, that was actually done by Allen Toussaint, the renowned Crescent City musician and songwriter. A young Toussaint cut a sprightly instrumental during one of his first recording sessions in 1960, opened the studio window, and smelled coffee. So he named it "Java," and trumpeter Al Hirt made the song a hit soon after.)

In nearly every city I've visited, there's a record store I've come to love. Can't imagine how I'd live without Waterloo Records in Austin, where the late local hero Doug Sahm gets the same amount of shelf-space that most stores would devote to Eminem. Or Boston's own Newbury Comics, which was a punk-identified comics store and indie-singles outlet before it became a small chain. Among those who've worked the counter at Newbury is Aimee Mann, who wasn't yet a star but carried herself like one. I well remember the dirty look she gave me when I handed her the just-released Genesis single "Mama"—a good record, dammit—and asked for a preview listen. I got less attitude from Sid Griffin, the former Long Ryders leader and an unsung hero of the alternative country movement, who used to work the counter at Rhino Records in Santa Monica. From Griffin I made an even less trendy purchase—the Bee Gees box set that came out in the early '90s. He rolled his eyes a bit, said, "Yeah, their early stuff was pretty good," and knocked a few bucks off the price.

In recent years I've been enamored of the Louisiana Music Factory, a collector's hotspot in New Orleans. It's not the only record store in the French Quarter, not even the only good one. The local big-chain outlets, Tower and Virgin, both do their bit to stock independent local CDs and import oldies collections. But neither has much vinyl, and neither has quite the same atmosphere.

There are few more picturesque places to put a record store than on Decatur Street, just two blocks upstream from the Mississippi River. Down the street to the south is an instant tourist magnet, the local branch of the nationwide music chain the House of Blues. To the east is a different sort of tourist magnet—a block's worth of strip clubs, with dancers hustling business from outside the doorways. Daiquiri bars sit on every corner, selling deceptively sweet Day-Glo concoctions that prove more dangerous than anything you'll get at home. Assorted street punks, panhandlers and off-duty vampires brush past you on the way in. As vices go, the idea of spending a week's pay on old vinyl starts to look awfully harmless.

The Music Factory sits right in the middle of this clutter like a great old album sitting in a messy living room. Like many good things in New Orleans, the Music Factory is a head-on collision of tourist culture and the real, indigenous stuff. During one of the city's festivals, Mardi Gras or the Jazz & Heritage Festival, the place will be packed with out-of-towners satisfying their Neville Brothers cravings, perhaps winding up there only because they stumbled onto this tiny homegrown store on the way to Tower. On a good day the owners would set up a keg behind the front desk, knowing that a free draft never hurt anybody's potential for impulse buying.

Nor does free music, and the store also provides its share of that. During festival days they squeeze a makeshift stage right between the bulging CD racks, the cash register and the bathroom. Plenty of local musicians have sold stacks of CDs by playing a live set for the crowds on festival days, so you might wind up bumping into one of the city's legends—and the aisles are narrow and crowded enough that I mean that literally. One day I did my part for the cause of music and art by letting Boozoo Chavis, the late accordionist who could rightly claim he invented zydeco music, cut ahead of me to use the bathroom.

I'd heard about the place via a CD by the Treme Brass Band, a street-parade outfit that hails from one of New Orleans's tougher neighborhoods. On this day they were joined onstage by a Japanese tourist that nobody's seen before or since. The man picked up a banjo and proceeded to sit in. Normally he'd be likely to get the bum's rush, but it turned out that he played well and knew the songs, so he stayed aboard for most of an hour-long set. As fate would have it, the performance made it to the group's next album, with the unrehearsed banjo parts left in. Last I heard, they were still trying to find the guy to pay him his royalties.

I had the good sense not to bring my banjo when I paid my first visit to the store. But I did make a point of filling my wallet beforehand, and headed down there single-mindedly. No desire to score a loaded daquiri, no time to grab a dozen oysters for the road, no temptation to duck into the strip clubs—well, maybe a quick glance. This day I was a man on a romantic quest. I had to find more of those old singles, preferably something I'd never heard of before. Even the band onstage didn't sway me as I pushed through the door, said a few quick hellos to faces I vaguely recognized, grabbed the obligatory free beer, and got to work. I walked past the CD racks that everyone was browsing, and made my way to the diehard's refuge—up the stairs and in a quiet, relatively deserted, library-like room—where the vinyl is kept.

In truth, much of their vinyl collection is nothing special, just multiple copies of those same REO Speedwagon and Styx albums that everybody had the sense to get rid of after they graduated high school. These are the records that nobody will admit to owning but, to judge from the sheer volume of the used copies that turn up, everybody did, even in cities that would theoretically be above all that. New Orleans may pride itself as the home of the Meters and Professor Longhair—a place where the world's funkiest jazz and R&B is there for the taking—but the awful truth is that the city harvested as many worn-out copies of *Frampton Comes Alive* as any other.

But tucked away on a lower shelf is the real deal: about two dozen boxes full of vintage 45s, every seven-inch they could find that has anything to do with New Orleans. Some of these records were retired from service in jukeboxes, some were probably buried deep in radio-station libraries, others were store copies that managed to last for thirty-plus years, shuffled from one store to another without being sold. So the original copies of that rowdy R&B that I'd come to love would wind up here, and some of the city's musical secrets would be in these very stacks.

The adrenalin races as I thumb through the piles of well-worn picture sleeves, weeding out the ordinary stuff—yes, Irma Thomas's "Time Is On My Side" is a great song, but only an amateur would still need a copy—and looking for the obscurities. So Dr. John recorded a football song for the New Orleans Saints, one that nobody outside the city ever heard? Good Lord, stash that one in my pile before anybody else comes across it. "Ape Man," a non-hit Aaron Neville single from the mid-'60s? Maybe not, because I already had the song on a CD. But something about that plain and fading yellow label—stamped with a simple, functional "Parlo Records, New Orleans LA"—had the inescapable feel of the '60s about it. Maybe some DJ encountered Neville's name for the first time on this very record—hell, maybe Neville himself brought it to the station. That possibility alone makes it worth the six dollars they're asking.

Next up, an ultra-obscure single by an '80s rock band, Li'l Queenie and the Percolators? Might have passed that one by, but in fact I'd recently been introduced to Queenie herself—a warm, exuberant woman who happened to show up at a party I'd been to. Maybe I'd run into her again, and the urge to tell her I'd just bought a record that she probably hadn't thought about in years proved too good to pass up.

I browsed further along the alphabet, and there it was, the treasure I'd been seeking: "Show Me Your Pretties" by Oliver "Who Shot the La La" Morgan. I gave myself a mental pat on the back for recognizing the artist's name—he's one of those one-shot regional artists who turned his sole national hit from the mid-'60s into his nickname. This particular tune was recorded years later. I'd heard it on a local radio station that specialized in New Orleans trivia, and recognized it as the kind of party record that we well-behaved Bostonians have trouble making: vaguely smutty, pure doggerel and pure abandon (let's just say that "pretties" is a radio-friendly rhyme for what he really wants to see). My head was already planning my next party tape—the songs I'd use to build the mood before this gem came on the sound system. "Is he really saying that?" some well-behaved guest would ask, and I'd smile knowingly.

I could get a pristine copy of "Pretties" for ten dollars, or a rather scratchy one with a beat-up sleeve for half that. Sounds like an easy decision, I thought as I stuck the clean copy into my pile. But hold on a minute: what sort of history did the scratchy one have, and how exactly did those scratches get there? This is a Mardi Gras song, so surely the owner hadn't listened to it sober. Maybe it was played at some society function as the debutantes got into costume. Or maybe it came from further downtown, as the festival kicked into high gear, the potions flowed and plenty of, er, pretties were being shown. So that explains the scratches, I thought. If this record was listened to in the proper spirit, nobody would have the presence of mind to make sure they were handling it by the edges. Couldn't let the thing sit in a dusty box forever; it needed to be the soundtrack for a few more parties.

I stuck the clean copy back and tucked the worn one under my arm. Now I could finally relax—after the records had
been paid for and my bag safely stowed away, of course. Now
I could say hello to the fellow collectors I'd avoided on my
way in, for fear they'd find the singles boxes before me.
Downstairs a swamp-rock band from bayou country had
taken the stage, somebody was buying a T-shirt with Professor Longhair's picture on it, and the city's musical history
was still being written and danced to. I knew I'd have a piece
of that history to call up anytime I gave "Show Me Your
Pretties" a spin.

A good afternoon's haul, but still nothing compared to
what the likes of Tefteller does to find records. While I was
poking through boxes of well-used singles, the truly devoted
were scavenging trunks and basements, and looking in unlikely towns like Port Washington, Wisconsin.

This city on the west shore of Lake Michigan—population at
last count: 9,338—is one of the last places you'd ever call a
blues hotbed, especially during the '20s and '30s. Unless you
know that this quiet, predominantly white, German town was
then home to a blues label that some would call the greatest
of all time: the Paramount Recording Company, which released 78s by Son House, Charley Patton, and Skip James—
essentially the cream of pre-war blues, the same records
that Robert Crumb and like-minded collectors are hoarding
today—along with seminal jazz sides by Louis Armstrong and
Jelly Roll Morton. Paramount was owned by the Wisconsin

Chair Company, which had a sideline in making phonograph cabinets. Many of its records were given away as bonuses for cabinet buyers. In fact, Paramount only jumped into jazz and blues after finding that its German and Mexican ethnic records weren't selling. Port Washington is only 110 miles from Chicago, with a railway joining the two cities, so its blues connection isn't all that farfetched. Today the city draws tourists with its historic lighthouses, but the site of Paramount is still unmarked.

"*The locals* were not fans of blues music," says Tefteller, whose Paramounts are the prizes of his collection. "Most residents of that area probably didn't know that blues were being recorded there, unless they were employed by the company. The singers were brought in on the inter-urban railway, they were recorded, put up in a hotel to spend the night, and sent home the next morning. They weren't even seen on the street—and given the times and the racial things, that was probably fine with the people of Port Washington."

Now picture a man with grey hair and moustache, prone to wearing a T-shirt marked "Record Collector," driving around this town, knocking on doors, chasing down senior citizens who might have old Paramounts in their attic. The Blind Joe Reynolds disc may have fallen into his lap by pure luck, but much of Tefteller's collecting has been more methodical. He's out to find records that haven't been collected yet, an enterprise that requires a willingness to travel, enough cash to throw around, and a lot of detective work. Forget about record stores and Internet sites, he says—that isn't where the real action is. "The obvious place where a novice will look is Salvation Army stores, goodwill stores, junk and antique shops. If you did enough of that, you would probably find something—but you'd be absolutely destroyed with expenses before you did. If you pulled into New Orleans or a good music town, the records may be there but you wouldn't find them just lying around. That's like winning the lottery—forget it, it's not gonna happen.

"And if you're looking for blues and R&B, you probably want to stay in the South—anywhere from Virginia to Florida, and down to Texas. It starts to dry out when you hit New Mexico. Arizona is pretty dry; Colorado is pretty bad. And you have to stay out of places where they were only into easy-listening pop, or polkas. I've been on too many wild goose chases to some basement in Iowa, where they'd tell you someone had a thousand 78s in their basement, and it would all be polka records. Or people will think they have a blues record because the word blues is in the song title. It could just as easily be some dumb dance band doing a song that has blues in the title."

You can't even do what Crumb did in the '60s, going into black neighborhoods and knocking on doors—especially if you want early 78s, which have now outlasted their original owners. "What was hard work in the '80s is really hard work now. You've got working against you the sheer expense of staying on the road, rental car fees, the cost of staying at cheap hotels. Whatever records were left on store shelves—Crumb and those guys already got them. You have to be a real good hound dog to sniff them out now. But"—he throws in a pregnant, James Bond-like pause—"I know how to do it."

So how do you find any records? You pull into the library and do research. You look up the names of disc jockeys through the decades, what vending companies were around, and who was in the music business. You find the record stores that have been around the longest, and start dropping the names you've just learned. "You're not looking for people who bought records, because they probably just got what was popular. You want people who were in the music business— the ones that have them just because they were able to take home a lot of records. I'd walk into the little mom-and-pop stores, usually the people who owned them were in their 60s, and I'd talk to them like I was an old-time customer—'You remember so-and-so who used to come in here?' If you talked enough about the business in their area, you could open the magical doors real quick. 'Do you have any old inventory in the basement? Do you have any put away at home? Can you put me in touch with the widow of this DJ?' I would do that constantly. And I'd get records where people said there were no records."

The raid on Port Washington was the peak of his sleuthing. Before hitting town, he called around and got himself written up in the local newspaper. He also called the radio stations and put the word out that he was looking for descendants of Paramount employees. The big haul came from a woman who called him, someone whose grandmother had stashed a bunch of records in a trunk. These included another uncollected Paramount, "My Buddy Blind Lemon" by King Solomon Hill. Best of all, the woman said the magic words: "I don't think Grandma ever played this one. She didn't like blues very much."

Tefteller is the first to admit that it's only a good, not a great record—but the payoff is that he's able to say that at all. The mystery that will remain is how much he paid for it. "I gave her quite a substantial amount of money. I told her it was an important record, that I'd make her very happy, and she was. For her it was free, a part of her inheritance, and she was glad to see it go to someone who appreciated it. And I do, and it's not leaving my house; there's no price for it now. You'll have to make that one up."

It's safe to say that nobody goes prospecting for records in Maine or Martha's Vineyard—maybe in 50 years when there's a market for Carly Simon's leftovers. The hotspots are places that once had a thriving independent music circuit. That still covers a good part of the country, since the South had its blues and jazz, the Northeast its doo-wop, and the Northwest its garage rock. Lightning struck twice in Seattle, once the "Louie Louie" capital of the world, and more recently the home of Sub Pop. "Everything got inflated during the time of Sub Pop mania," says Steve Turner of Mudhoney, referring to the label that broke Nirvana along with his own band. "There's still good records here, even though Japanese tourists keep coming over and buying them. But that's alright, because I've sold a few myself, and now I know where to look when I go to Japan."

One motherlode that's still being tapped is that of '70s funk. The giants of this genre—James Brown, George Clinton, the Meters—seem to get rediscovered every year, not least because a generation of rappers have sampled their licks. But though Brown and Clinton made more records than most ordinary human beings, the well is bound to run dry sometime. At the other end of the notoriety scale are the regional funk bands who made one or two singles in the '70s, played a bunch of parties and disappeared. With rappers hungry for new samples and fans looking for more grooves, it's no surprise that the search for those records is something of a scavenger hunt.

One of the big winners on this count is producer Eothan "Egon" Alapatt, whose funk and hip-hop label Stones Throw is the kind of enterprise collectors love. No matter how much you know about funk, you probably didn't know anything about the records he's unearthed (though his 2001 compilation, *The Funky 16 Corners*, offers a neat crash course). These were fly-by-night bands under the Brown/Meters spell, most of whom never got as far as an album, none of whom ever got close to national recognition. Tracks like the Ebony Rhythm Band's "Soul Heart Transplant" are just a little more gonzo than anything that would have made the radio.

Finding records like these is what Alapatt lives for. He swears he chose to attend Vanderbilt University in Nashville

during the early '90s, specifically because it was convenient
to so many record-intensive cities. "Any free weekend I had
I was going into Indianapolis, Little Rock, Memphis." Not to
mention to the Louisiana Music Factory, where he scavenged
the same boxes of 45s that I did. But he found the clue that
led to a bigger score. "Most of it was just stuff that I'd seen
before. But I found one record that I knew I was into: 'Do
the Cissy' by Charlie Simmons & the Royal Imperials, that
one's topnotch. But I'm looking at the record, and inside the
dead wax someone had taken a marker and written the initials
'TW.' I asked the guy at the counter what that means and he
said it was a guy in the country who brings records in, but
he couldn't give me his number. I finally talked him into it—
told him I'd come all the way from Nashville—and it led me
to a record store in the projects that had been closed since
1990. The Jamaicans had already been there a few times
looking for 45s. And the place was a freakin' goldmine, it was
just chock full of the funk."

The word goldmine is appropriate, since most of the people holding those funk nuggets know what they're worth.
"Let's say that I'm trying to find these records, so I can reissue them and do it legally, giving money to the guys in the
bands. And maybe somebody else wants to hoard them or to
bootleg them, and we're both trying to call members of the
same band. Some of these people want to find one hundred
and fifty copies of a record, hold onto most of them, and
maybe put five in circulation to keep the value up. A lot of
these older dudes did a funk record or two and didn't record

anything else, and maybe someone's trying to get the record from them, saying that it isn't worth anything. Meanwhile the guy is just happy that somebody wanted to hear his music. Which is why I'm hoping I can get there first."

Besides, we probably wouldn't have heard "Soul Heart Transplant" if he hadn't gotten it pumping again and put it back into circulation. "No joke, that one took years. We're talking trips to Indianapolis, staying in twenty-five dollar hotels when it's one hundred degrees, sun beating down on your head. It was on a relatively well known Indianapolis label, but it was the one piece nobody could find. Turned out the bass player's mother had just died, and he tells me, 'I think she may have a copy or two in there, but I'm not going through her stuff'—How frustrating is that? Finally I find a dude in the band who tells me, 'I have it, but my friend Butchie played on that record, so I can't possibly send it to you.' And I tell him, no, you're wrong—I know who's on those records, and Butchie played on a different one. When he figured I was right, we finally got it. Some of those guys have made a lot of money off me."

As a relatively young guy into a relatively young kind of music, Alapatt figures he has years of sleuthing ahead. "A friend of mine just got back from Minneapolis, and he got some pretty heavy records. Out of nowhere he pulls a record with no address and no label information, but it's by the Black Conspirators, and this record sounds like Jesus. And I'm thinking, how did I miss this one? It may have come from somebody who brought a collection in from Gary, Indiana.

So we're gonna go down there and make some more rounds."

For the sake of my own collection, I can only hope he succeeds. If the heart transplant worked so well, there's got to be a "Soul Quadruple Bypass" out there somewhere.

chapter 9

VALLEY OF THE STRANGE

*S*o *you* think that you own the worst, most unlistenable record ever made? Well, you're probably wrong. Unless you can honestly say that you own an entire disc's worth of a rabbit screaming.

There's no obvious reason why this record should exist, but it does. Two full sides (only a single, thankfully) of a bunny shrieking its furry little head off. Divided into parts one and two—to increase its commercial potential, no doubt—"Distress Cries of the Cottontail" adds up to a good six minutes. How they got the critter to stand in front of the mike for that long is lost to history, so is the question of whether the rabbit received its fair share of the royalties. But it does stand as two sides of the most godawful yowls ever inflicted on vinyl. At the very least, it must have been highly influential in the career of Yoko Ono.

The keeper of this artifact is Greg Hillegas of Los Angeles, a man who has no trouble getting rid of his guests after a party. "That record is truly horrible, and that's exactly what I've used it for. It makes people really uncomfortable, like hearing the baby cry in *Eraserhead*. The theory is that if you hear a rabbit screaming there must be a fox nearby, so I'm guessing that this record was made for fox hunters, to familiarize them with that sound."

A video game designer of some note (with the PlayStation II game "Medal of Honor" among his recent credits), Hillegas has never been fox hunting in his life. But he is part of a growing group of collectors who scoop up what most of us would consider the dregs—the leftovers, the truly bizarre, and the just plain lousy.

Truly bizarre records just aren't easy to find nowadays. The music on the radio may be blander now than it was in the '60s, but the average tolerance for transgressive music is far higher. The Velvet Underground finally became rock stars a couple decades after breaking up. Frank Zappa came into music as a scary radical, and went out as a respected American institution. The Residents are still mighty strange, but haven't shocked anybody for years. And you were weirded out by the first Devo album in high school? Forget it—those guys are doing cartoon soundtracks these days.

Yesterday's loners and oddballs have become today's cult

heroes and commercial soundtracks. For proof, just visit my local coffeehouse, where I can introduce you to a bunch of twenty-two-year-olds who groove daily to the music of the late English folk poet Nick Drake. Credit that to a Volkswagen commercial using "Pink Moon," an ominous song that Drake recorded near the end of his short life. It should have been on the radio thirty years ago, but now it's in the hearts of people who weren't born when it was recorded. And I'm proud to be driving a Volkswagen.

Even the longtime outsiders have come inside. For decades there was one record that vinyl junkies could clutch as proof of truly adventurous taste: *Philosophy of the World* by the Shaggs. The story of that disc is almost common knowledge by now. Three New Hampshire sisters, endowed with great emotion and severely gypped in musical skills, were coaxed by their dad into becoming a '60s rock group. By any rational standard, the girls had no business picking up instruments— their random gropes at rhythm and melody frustrate all notions of musical logic. Yet the record's warmth and naiveté somehow transcend its ineptness, and various hipsters including Zappa and NRBQ have championed it over the years. No reason to do so anymore, however. The cult's grown so much that the album has since been reissued on RCA, *New Yorker* writer Susan Orlean managed to track down the reclusive sisters for an interview, and Tom Hanks optioned the rights for a movie.

Heard today, *Philosophy* sounds like just another good '60s pop record, its quirks now part of the standard vocabulary. A similar fate may yet catch up with Jandek, the Texas odd-

ball who's been making home recordings for two decades—
all graced with similar covers, all full of screechy, atonal
songs about the perennially pathetic state of his love life. It's
less charming than the Shaggs, yet he's made nearly three
dozen albums so far and even reissued the old ones on CD,
so somebody's got to be buying them. Figure that he's sold a
few hundred copies of each disc, and he's likely moved as
many copies overall as Mick Jagger did on his last turkey of
a solo album.

But when you've got all that esoterica, you've only scratched
the surface. All the above were still made by people who are,
more or less, musicians. Which means they have an edge
over, say, the GE Silicone Division when it made an album
called *Got to Investigate Silicone*. Or the Brother sewing machine company, whose aural introduction to a new automatic
knitter took up two entire records in the mid-'6os. Yes, a
double concept album about a sewing machine—the commercial equivalent of *Tales From Topographic Oceans* by Yes.
Somehow, art-rock parallels seem to abound in this genre.
Consider an album that the Emerson company put out to cel-
ebrate a new vacuum cleaner, *The Eight Seasons of Chromalux*—
an Emerson, Lake & Palmer album title waiting to happen, if
ever there was one.

The cult classic of this genre is *The Name of the Game*, a
full-blown, Broadway-style production of a record that featured future television stars David Hartman and Loretta Swit.
It just happens that every song on the album was about *Lis-*

terine, which apparently commissioned the album to be handed out at a convention. Having put in years of scouring thrift stores and garage sales, Hillegas scammed this masterpiece for a mere dollar—a small price to pay for an album that includes a rousing showstopper about the thrill of placing mouthwash on supermarket shelves. (The perpetrators were the celebrated songwriting team of Kander & Ebb, just a few years before their success with *Cabaret* and *Chicago*.) "My guess is that it was actually performed as a musical—there are pictures from the show on the back cover. I believe it was produced at a big, prostitute-heavy hotel in St. Louis, to pay them back for all their hard work selling the product."

You can't write this off as a totally worthless record—Broadway historians along with kitsch connoisseurs might be after it—but it is the kind of thing nobody thought to look for until recently. Beyond the realm of anything considered desirable lurk whole ranks of records: commercial extravaganzas like those above; instructional records of all stripes; and the dreaded "celebrities singing" genre—starting with those Leonard Nimoy and William Shatner albums, still classic in the genre of pop records by random personalities who really should have known better.

Further along the edge, one finds the singing ventriloquist's dummy named Little Marcy, perhaps the most notorious example of Christian good-heartedness gone terribly wrong. The creation of Marcy Tigner, an amateur musician and self-taught ventriloquist from Wichita, Little Marcy made dozens

of albums that actually sold respectably in the '60s, and she
was still cranking them out as recently as 1982. All examine
the complexities of Bible teachings as they might be interpreted by, well, a ventriloquist's dummy. It always comes
down to a chirpy little song and few spoonfuls of sugar. Some
have claimed there's a disturbing sexual undercurrent to the
Little Marcy records, and when you hear the helium-voiced
Marcy serenading her cat with a song called "I Love Little
Pussy," you do have to wonder.

"There's tons of ventriloquist Christian records," Hillegas
assures me. "They come from a time when there seemed to
be no irony. The word gay, meaning happy, turns up a lot."
The real question is why a non-Christian over six would want
to hear these, much less own them. "I'm fascinated most by
things that I can't believe were ever made. Bovine anthrax
medicine records, heart disease records, you name it. Some
drug company produces a record of the human heart beating—you have to wonder who the audience was. Some of
these records seem the obvious worst idea ever, yet they were
mass produced, they look like any other kind of record. For
a long time, I felt the need to save this, just to make sure it
all survived. A lot of this stuff is so ridiculous that it would
be sold for landfill if somebody didn't collect it. Now that
there is a vogue for this sort of thing, I'm feeling more that
the pressure is off."

It's only within, roughly, the past fifteen years that these
marginal records have become collectible artifacts. A small
handful of factors are likely to blame. One is the Rhino Records's "Golden Throats" compilation series, four CDs (so far)

of '60s pop hits interpreted by out-of-place celebrities (Jack "Dragnet" Webb's somber oration of Otis Redding's "Try a Little Tenderness" may be the classic of this genre). Another was the underground publisher Re/Search's "Incredibly Strange Music" series of books and CDs, which introduced the punk/alternative audience to the joys of thriftshop records and pulled a few obscure careers (notably that of space-age mambo king Esquivel) out of the fire. Even Little Marcy put in an appearance on one of their CDs.

A more famous godfather of junkshop music is David Letterman. The segment "Dave's Record Collection" was a recurring feature on his show for more than a decade, drawing yuks from quick snippets of silly thrift-store discs. But no, it wasn't Dave who actually owned those records. That honor went to Steve Young, a staff writer who took over "Dave's Record Collection" when he joined the show in 1990 and oversaw the segment for the next decade. During that time, Young had what every collector dreams of: A job that required him to hang out in record stores and a budget to bring home the goods.

"Usually I'd meet dealers who'd give me things they had shoved in the back room for years and years. I've still got a lot of 'em right here," Young says, thumbing through a pile in his New York office. "Let's see: *Talking to Your Plants. Step Up Your Selling: The Art of Carpet Salesmanship*—that was a good one. And here we have *What You Always Wanted to Know About Bedwetting*—this record makes the hard-to-believe claim that over one million men were discharged from the U.S. Armed Forces during World War II for that problem. You'd think a lot of these records couldn't be real, but they were. Here's *Music to Install Gas Vents By*—apparently you're supposed to use a lot of New Orleans jazz while installing them."

Young says that about a half-dozen small shops in Greenwich Village provided most of his material. "You're looking for ten to fifteen seconds of unintentionally funny audio with a cover that Dave could hold up, say some smart-ass remark, and move on to the next one. We always had good luck with Mr. Rogers. Sometimes it was just as simple as a cheap joke. You can take an exercise record and use a clip that goes 'In! Out!'—that's pretty much throwing red meat to the audience." However, some of the more obvious red-meat moments got the axe. "There was a *Breast Enlargement Through Hypnosis* record that I was sure Dave was going to like, but he turned that one down. He thought it would inflame the yahoos in the audience to scream and shout too much. You want a big response, but not a certain kind of big response."

"Dave loved the singing celebrities," he recalls. Those include a few that have escaped being reissued so far—notably the disco single that Farrah Fawcett made in the '70s, and the psychedelic album that Joe Pesci made under an assumed name a decade earlier. And the Imelda Marcos rendition of "Feelings," recorded to assist her sister's low-level singing career.

The legal logistics, I suggest, must have been a nightmare. "Actually we didn't worry too much about that. Playing something for fifteen seconds gives you a lot more latitude. We'd send everything over to the CBS legal department, who'd either get permission or take the calculated risk that we could get away with it. But we certainly used a lot that were so obscure that we didn't have to worry about anyone bothering us, like the ones about how to install a faucet in your bathroom sink. I don't recall being told not to use anything except for a Disney record—they demand five thousand dollars for ten seconds of material, so we figured we could do it without Mickey Mouse." The "Record Collection" was quietly retired in 2001, when it became evident that the supply of celebrity records was running out, and that not a lot of dictators seem to be recording "Feelings" anymore.

Young's own collecting habits aren't far from the kind immortalized on the show. He also has a jones for those industrial-musical albums, which remain some of the rarest collectibles of all. Most people who had copies tended to throw them out; but at least three groups of people are after them, the serious Broadway historians, the people who want to hear something ridiculous, and then folks like Young and Hillegas, who think the stuff is really good. "It's social history, a bit of Americana. I mean, *Got to Investigate Silicone* has a song about the benefits of silicone, and it's six minutes long. That really taxes the limits of human creativity."

This trend went further than most people realize. Celebrated musical comic Allen Sherman, of "Hello Muddah Hello Faddah" fame, recorded an entire album about paper cups when the Scott company commissioned one in 1966. "It's an extremely well produced little slab of corporate propaganda," is Young's verdict. The mid-'60s would bring revues with titles like *Chrysler-Plymouth à Go-Go*, and songs that borrowed hippie terminology. (Westinghouse joined the fray in 1969 with a tune called "Power Flower"—its employees weren't just selling refrigerators, they were working together to "make the power flower.") "I've spent a fair amount of time tracking down composers. They don't get a lot of people asking about that diesel show they did in 1965. This was its own, secret little genre. The other strange thing is that if I listen to enough of these songs, I'm suddenly walking around singing about typewriters and insurance."

Like any good advertising, these records seem to carry some persuasive power. Few people even know about them, but those who do feel compelled to track them down. "I don't feel like I chose to collect them," Young says. "I feel like they chose me."

Even after meeting these collectors, I still suspected that I hadn't found the most absurd limits of recorded music. That search led me to the edge of Manhattan, where Paul Major and his amazing collection reside.

A devotee of all that's strange and homemade, Major has turned his obsession into a cottage industry. He does brisk enough business at record shows to afford a shared Manhattan apartment, and his own label, Parallel World, has reissued a few of his fringe discoveries. His collection is something of a refuge for oddballs: laughable lounge bands, religious zealots, and lonesome losers all find a place in his collection. And

Major collects this stuff for the strangest of reasons: because it's what he prefers to listen to.

"Some people say it's crap, I say it's brilliant genius expression," he proclaims as he lights a cigarette. Now forty-six, Major has the longhaired look of a longtime rocker, after a casual glance you might mistake him for Derek Smalls of Spinal Tap. Like the Louisiana natives who formed the Residents, the Kentucky-born Major has a down-home accent that seems at odds with his musical explorations. Thanks to his roommate's high-level record-label job, the house is hung with gold records by the likes of Tina Turner and Paula Abdul. So when his favorite records echo off those walls, you've got to figure that the misfits are getting their revenge.

Vinyl junkiedom hit him at an early age, and his diverse collection bears the mark of many tastes and eras. Mainstream names like Santana and Traffic sit side by side with punk and new wave staples. But the bizarre side of his taste can perhaps be traced to a quirk in radio programming. As a preteen he lived in St. Louis, where local radio programmers were more receptive to oddball singles than most. He can remember the Silver Apples's "Oscillations"—an early electronic rocker much admired by today's avant-gardists—as a genuine AM-radio hit. Thanks to a local Kmart with a large bargain bin, he was able to pick up the Silver Apples's album and loads of others for 33 cents apiece, which gave him room to build both a collection and an obsession. He moved cross-country with his collection, through a college spell in St. Louis, a marriage in New Hampshire, and finally a move to New York that began in the West Village. "You can't imagine what it was like to carry six thousand albums up six floors on Bleecker and Macdougal," he notes. During college years he played in one of St. Louis's first punk bands, the Moldy Dogs, But his own tastes were running toward the fringes of psychedelia and beyond.

And once psychedelia sounds normal, you're on the way down a slippery slope. "You know how it is—you collect a lot of psychedelia and you start thinking, 'This stuff is great, but how many versions of "Gloria" can I hear?' " he notes. In a quest for something deeper and weirder, he latched onto Jandek, and the Shaggs, ahead of the crowd. But nothing quite struck the ideal chord, until Kenneth Higney came into his life.

Think of the buzz you got the first time you heard the Beatles, Nirvana, or whoever first launched you into musical heaven. That's how Major felt when he heard the tuneless screech of this New Jersey truck driver. It happened innocently enough, when Major was booking a club and Higney, who had designs on a legitimate career in country music, sent a copy of his album. The cover is enough to let you know that something is up. It's a close-up shot of the artist, who wears his hair at shoulder-length in the familiar outlaw style of Kris Kristofferson. But the eyes show just enough of a manic glare to make you a little nervous that this guy's on the road. As for the music, let's say it's enough to give you second thoughts about ever taking a Jersey highway. "This is a glimpse of someone's worldview," Major explains. "Some people are going to hear the wrong notes and say 'so bad it's great,' but to me it's straight-out good—it's all wrong musically, but emotionally it's perfect. The bad music is all the bland normal stuff."

Imagine that the late disc jockey Wolfman Jack had tried to style himself as a dark country balladeer, and you'd have some insight into Higney's approach. For starters, he rhymes "home" with "roam," a too-obvious rhyme that has apparently replaced "fire/desire" as the last refuge of the poetically challenged. For another, the man couldn't carry a tune in a souped-up semi. The opening "Nightrider" is a Skynyrd-type rocker gone terribly wrong. Rhythmically, it's a train wreck, as the drums and guitar struggle bravely to find some common ground. Like most of his songs, it ends with a glaringly ominous lyric—"Night rider, sleep with a peaceful mind/ Knowing you're gonna keep the world safe from your own kind"—that comes out of nowhere, upends whatever mood the song already had, and makes you fear for the artist's sanity. Not to mention your own, if you play the thing enough.

I cast a guilty look at Major, having broken into yuks over one of his favorite records. But that's fine, he's seen it before— and to him it's a miracle that this record exists. After all, you or I could have made this album, but we didn't. Some notion of good taste or self-respect got in the way. "What I love is that someone like this was so driven to get a record out," he says. "It's like trying to get into someone's head, getting a glimpse of their worldview. It's a masterpiece, for all the wrong reasons." As it turns out, Major has tracked Higney down and now owns a whole box of his albums, which fetch a few hundred bucks apiece. "He's a totally mild-mannered guy, and he's getting a little bit of celebrity status." As for the fact that Higney's only semi-famous because his record is so bad it's great . . . Well, Higney doesn't ask and Major doesn't tell. "That's the hard part, when that syndrome comes up. People think it's a pretty heavy record, but not necessarily for the same reason that the artist thinks. It's the discrepancy between what they intended and what they really are."

The artists Major admires haven't always been so friendly to his advances. He once, for example, tried to track down a gentleman named Palmer Rockey, whose story is a bit unique. A late-'70s lounge lizard from Dallas, Rockey enjoyed an active social life, befriending enough high-society ladies who were willing to sink money into his creative interests. These apparently included both sadomasochism and the occult. Having charmed enough money out of his patrons, Rockey produced a film called *Scarlet Love*, whose scenes are rumored to include a dream sequence featuring a woman strapped to a wheel covered with razor blades. All Major's been able to ascertain is that it played for one night in Dallas, with those warmhearted ladies in attendance, and Rockey promptly skipped town the next morning.

The soundtrack album is a little easier to find, and it does support any bizarre rumors about the film. Sure, lots of people can write songs about violent sexual practices and the occult—but on a disco record? Appropriately enough, the blurry face on the cover has Manson's intense stare and Elvis's pompadour. One song rhymes "666" with "Sex-sex-sex"; another finds Palmer intoning—in the most ominous voice he can manage—"When a star beauty gives you a glance, all you wanna do is sing and dance." Prevailing on friends who had access to government tracking files, Major was elated to find Palmer Rockey living in California. But as soon as Major called the number and mentioned *Scarlet Love*, the voice on the other end replied "Don't ever call me about that again," and slammed the phone down.

He was more successful with Peter Grudzien, a Nashville character whose songs combine lopsided twang, quasi-classical interludes, and some of the clumsier gay innuendo in lyrical history. His masterstroke may be "White Trash Hillbilly Trick," a tale of sexual depravity sung in a voice that sounds like a John Wayne imitation. "This is someone who's still pursuing a career in mainstream country music," Major points out. Convinced he was hearing a masterpiece that Nashville wouldn't recognize, he managed to earn enough of Grudzien's trust to license a CD for his own label—no small feat, since the singer is convinced that he's being pursued by the CIA.

During their negotiations, Major received his share of 4 A.M. phone calls from Grudzien, who suspected him of working for the Feds. "For awhile he refused to send me any tapes. He believed that the government was trying to intercept his mail, and downgrade the quality of his music." (This, of course, assumes that they'd be capable of downgrading it any further.) Nonetheless, Major released the CD—*The Unicorn*—which has even earned a mention in the *New York Times* (in an article on "Untamed Sounds from Well Beyond the Margins"). The CD booklet includes an early-'60s photo of Grudzien standing next to Johnny Cash—and like the famous photo of Elvis with Richard Nixon, it's hard to say who looks the more wasted. Despite his conspiracy theories, Grudzien is still a free man and his music remains untainted. But alas, as yet Garth Brooks has shown no interest in covering "Hunky-Honky" or "Candy-Ass Lover."

If anything can make Palmer Rockey or Peter Grudzien sound reassuring, it's another record in Major's archive: a little number called *Sammy Squirrel Teaches the Multiplication Tables*. Behind this innocent title—crudely stamped in red script onto a plain white cover—is one of the most disturbing records I've ever heard. As usual with records of this ilk, its origins are a mystery. If this is a study guide for schoolkids, just try explaining the address on the cover: "The Metaphysical Motivational Institute, Drawer 400, Ruidoso, NM." Yes, the odds are good that we've stumbled onto some kind of mind control disguised as math. "They had to be using this as a trance record of some kind," Major offers, and notes that even he hasn't sat through the whole thing. "It's only going to take you a few seconds to realize where this one is coming from."

The voice on the record is supposed to be one of those cute squirrel or chipmunk voices, except that it's sped up just a little too much, to the point where it's more than a little creepy—the sonic equivalent of Chucky the killer doll. "Anyone can learn the multiplication tables. All you have to do is listen to me recite them . . . over and over again." Those last four words have a sinister overtone that's impossible to miss. Adding to the effect is a low-budget rhythm track that runs through the record, I'm guessing it's someone tapping a teaspoon onto a frying pan. "Two times two is four. Two times two is four. Two times two is FOUR." We skip ahead a bit, to where Sammy is intoning the three-times tables in exactly the same tone, but we don't have the gumption to go any further. Neither of us is sure that the squirrel doesn't start giving instructions on how to dismember your neighbors. (I can see the Ruidoso headlines already: "Depraved Neighbor Claims, 'I Did It For Sammy'!")

Time for some good clean fun, and what could be cleaner than the Catholic Church in the early '70s? Try casting your mind back to those days, when cultural quirks like *Godspell* and *Jesus Christ Superstar* are giving Jesus a newer, hipper image. Woodstock is over, hippie-dom is starting to settle down, quasi-religious records like "Put Your Hand in the Hand" and "One Toke Over the Line" are coming on the radio, and it looks like God might be the next big thing. Christian rock is with us to this day, through the piously popular Creed and their various clones.

But maybe the world just wasn't ready for the Click Kids, a group that lent new meaning to the term "God-awful." Major produces a cover that immediately snags my love for '60s/ early-'70s kitsch: the kids' fashion sense would best be described as "early Brady Bunch," the looks on their faces are impossibly wholesome for a '60s rock band, and the kicker is that they're standing on a bus spray-painted with the words "Jesus is a Soul Man." And they sound exactly like you'd expect such a group to sound: Gentle, tuneful, and gloriously clueless. In fact, I'm tempted to form a band just so I can cover "Happy Happy Christians," a song that no jaded modern artist could possibly write. Taking death-defying leaps into the high register, the frontman chirps "We believe Jesus died to save the world from sin," to an inappropriately jolly tune. During the guitar solo, the lead player inadvertently quotes "Anchors Aweigh," probably the only lick he could think of at the time. Light and folkish, it sounds remarkably like early Talking Heads without the irony—the Click Kids's naiveté was absolutely unforced. If nothing else, this band should have been the musical rulers of its hometown. Besides, how much competition could there have been in Clatskanie, Oregon?

Maybe I'm not ready to follow Major into the dark realm of Kenneth Higney and Palmer Rockey, but this one's right up my alley. There's an open-hearted quality in a lot of '60s music that excuses any amount of ineptness, and openhearted ineptness is what the Click Kids were all about. If it's a choice between the whiny Jesus-metal of Creed or the goofy warmth of this stuff from three decades earlier, then give me that old-time religion.

Our final stop may be the most unlikely place of all: The Holiday Inn in Salem, Oregon. That's where the act known as Silk & Silver recorded its one and only album on August 13, 1976. This, Major explains, is one of the many oddities that came out of cocktail lounges around the country. Every cheap motel had a house band, and far too many of them were tempted to immortalize their acts. This, of course, led to multiple versions of the same songs. "My favorite is when the groups attempt to do 'MacArthur Park.' Nobody can do that last high note at the end, and everybody has a different way to avoid it." Silk & Silver didn't succumb to that particular temptation, but their disc does contain the least promising biography ever to appear on a rock album: "Working at the local plywood mills provided the funds for Del to obtain his B.S. in sociology from the University of Oregon. The insurance career followed."

Silk & Silver's lasting gift to the world is an Elton John medley that proves one thing: nobody sounds sillier than an insurance salesman from Oregon trying to imitate a sexually ambiguous Englishman. Indeed, when he goes for the falsetto notes in "Rocket Man," it sounds like he's being goosed with a watermelon.

Yet there's a certain *joie de vivre* in this performance that you won't hear in Elton's original, and it's the sound that Major quests for: music as a spontaneous outpouring, unhampered by any notions of commerciality, quality or good taste. Am I tempted to forego all future trips to Memphis and New Orleans and instead make a musical pilgrimage to Salem, Oregon? Maybe so, if it will help get the damn squirrel out of my head.

CHAPTER TEN

33⅓   L.P

OUR FAVORITE SHOPS

(CHAPTER/TEN)

10

*E*very *vinyl* junkie of a certain age went to that same record department, they just found it in a different store in a different city. Long before the Internet supposedly brought everybody together, we were getting the same signals in different cities. It could have been Big Scott's in the Bronx or a family-run store in the Midwest, but the record department was basically the same. And which part of the store you gravitated to could say a lot about where you went later in life. There was a time, for instance, when I wouldn't go near an early Frank Zappa album, *Weasels Ripped My Flesh* because it had the grisliest cover art I'd ever seen: a grinning guy using a bloodthirsty rodent for a shaving razor. Meanwhile, in another part of New York, a preteenage

Thurston Moore was buying that album for the very same reason.

"Records like that always drew me in," says Moore. "There were records in the store that I always gravitated toward. I'd see something like *Weasels Ripped My Flesh* and think, 'Well, this is really something that you don't see everywhere. What is this? What's going on here?' It was a wild hippie, youth-culture kind of thing, and I wasn't of the age where it was my culture, it was something older. I had an older brother who influenced me in record collecting, he'd stack his records on top of his dresser, vertically. Even though he wasn't real hardcore, he started buying records before me and got me interested. He had maybe twenty of them, things like *Beggars Banquet* and *Abbey Road*, some Jefferson Airplane. It was so cool to see them stacked up like that – I was think-ing, 'Man, in about a year those are going to be stacked up to the ceiling.' I was already collecting comic books, so I had collector fever before records. I liked the organizational aspect of it. I have that quirk where everything has to be filed and organized."

His band, Sonic Youth, went on to produce its share of beautifully scary album covers, to say nothing of the music inside—and that die was likely cast when Moore brought his first records home. "I could only afford them every now and then. The first was *In-a-Gadda-da-Vida* (by Iron Butterfly), maybe in 1971. Now, that isn't a great record, but it is a weird, dark record in its way. Records were three dollars in the local Woolworth's, and I could tell by looking that it was going to be a heavy record. It almost didn't matter what the music was, you could go home and study the vinyl and the grooves." As anyone who bought the thing will attest, the side-long title track of *In-a-Gadda-da-Vida* had a long stretch of alternating loud/soft sections with a lengthy drum solo, which meant that the vinyl had a range of dense gray and sleek black shades: a perfect disc for extended groove-gazing.

A record with a three-dimensional cover was even better, and the Rolling Stones provided one. Moore wasn't the first to buy *Their Satanic Majesties Request* on the basis of the sleeve alone. "I wasn't even sure whose record it was. My mom said, 'Who's it by?' and I didn't know. I thought it might have been the Rolling Stones but the script on the cover was so weird, and I didn't want to be wrong. That's another frightening record musically. Unlike *In-a-Gadda-da-Vida*, I thought it was really fascinating. But I'm pretty sure I got it for the cover, the fact that it looked so arcane in the face of all those other records. It was one of those little bastions of unknown information, and I was super-intrigued by it."

My own first record store wasn't even a record store. It was a small corner of a Montgomery Ward department store, out on an industrial park near an IBM plant. It occupied the furthest corner of the store; to get there you had to pass through the long stretches of kitchenware and garden hoses. When it got close to Christmas they'd set up an expanded toy section just next to the records—the bright colors from the holiday spreads blending nicely with the psychedelic album jackets next door—and in my preteen years I'd have no qualms about hanging there for hours at a time.

The back cavern of a big store was an appropriate place to tuck a department that held so many secrets. The atmosphere of the place would change every couple of weeks, when they'd put a new half-dozen albums into the front display. It was a dull week when they'd make a gesture for the parents and put some Robert Goulet records up there. If there were more people than usual, it would probably mean that the Beatles had decided to release something. But I'd already become partial to a few lesser-known bands that I'd either seen on TV or read about in teen magazines (in the era when *16* or *Tiger Beat* might have the Doors and the Monkees on the same page, with Jim Morrison and Micky Dolenz striking some variation of the same soulful pose), so you'd find me in the corners thumbing through the neglected treasures: Paul Revere & the Raiders, who were mean as the Stones but nearly as catchy as the Beatles, and had far better costumes than either, were my cult heroes of choice. I was partial to an album called *Revolution!*, which showed the five Raiders in their preferred costumes—Revolutionary War by way of Carnaby Street—pouring tea on the porch of a house that looked like one of the many old-world houses in the quiet, dull patch of upstate New York where I lived. Of course, it was anyone's guess what that tea was spiked with, and it looked like the Raiders were on a mission to liven up my sleepy rural existence.

I wasn't allowed to buy more than an album a month, but the covers were nearly as good. Who needed to hear the music when you could gawk at the first Mamas & the Papas album, with the four group members crouched in a bathtub, barely suggesting sexual issues that we twelve-year-olds had yet to figure out? For that matter, I can thank Blind Faith for the first naked female body I ever saw depicted. The record racks had their good guys and bad guys—there were the odd Frank Zappa discs, the scary faces that scowled at you from the cover of *We're Only In It For the Money*, to fuel your budding cynicism. But most of all, there were those splashy, flowery-colored album covers. It could be a legit classic like the Beach Boys's *Wild Honey*, or something trivial like the Sunshine Company, but there would be those trippy colors, twelve square inches of Day-Glo radiating peace and love. Seems silly now, but at the time they at least promised that there would be more to life than kitchenware and garden hoses.

If you were ten when the '60s counterculture peaked, you were 20 when punk rock hit and set off a new wave of collecting. This time it wasn't your older brother or sister's culture, it was your own. And you didn't find the records in the department stores your parents frequented, but at a funkier spot in your own neighborhood. Punk rock was fuelled by a certain us-vs.-them mentality. You couldn't hear the new music on the big radio stations or buy it at Caldor's, so you'd discover a college station and an independent store.

For me it was Main Street Records in Northampton, which occupied part of the second floor of a hippie-esque mini-mall. There was a place that sold organic perfumes on the first floor, another had natural Chinese food. Main Street was a glorified clubhouse where every local student with a music jones would meet up on Saturday afternoons. On anniversary weekends they'd break out free champagne, which caused many an impromptu shopping spree. But they had the records you really wanted; nobody from the mall chains was going to send an order to England for the new Gang of Four single. One day before Christmas 1979, the first import copies of the Clash's *London Calling* showed up at Main Street before any of my gang knew it was coming (the American one wouldn't come out for another two months). It was perfect fodder for your bohemian lifestyle, or at least for your college radio show. One tasteless punk single I picked up, "Sit On My Face, Stevie Nicks" by the Rotters, was enough to keep the phone calls coming for weeks. To paraphrase an old Tom Lehrer album: Of all the songs I ever played on college radio, this was the one I got the most requests not to.

At that point living in Connecticut, Thurston Moore went to New York to find one of those stores, in the heart of Greenwich Village. "What happened with punk was that certain stores were devoted specifically to it. Bleecker Bob's on Macdougal Street was the church of buying punk-rock records. I remember being there when 'New Rose' [by the Damned] came out, and 'Anarchy in the UK' on a seven-inch. The owner would fly over to England and bring records back personally, and you would just buy everything regardless of who the artist was. It wasn't until 1977 that I felt I was buying things that were involved with who I was directly—The Ramones, Patti Smith and Television were all older than me, but I knew it was closer to me personally. Even though I wasn't hanging out on the Bowery, there was a certain vibe going on that I could catch; the bands were playing and I could actually see them. It wasn't like trying to listen to the Allman Brothers, or ELP, who were way beyond my age and experience."

Punk rock was full of ironies, not the least of which was that this anti-capitalist movement brought record collecting back with a vengeance. The landmark English punk single, the Sex Pistols's "Anarchy in the UK," was also an instant collectible, since it was banned and withdrawn by the time most Americans heard about it. Later came the Stiff label—home of Elvis Costello, the Damned, and Ian Dury—which fueled collectors' fever by screwing with label design, scratching secret messages into the run-out grooves, and immediately deleting the odd single to create a rarity. And if you cared about such things, the music was also really good.

As Moore notes, '50s and '60s collectibles were created by accident. Some rare performance or unique label design would get issued without much thought and the item would get discovered later. But by the time new wave happened, people had had enough "historical resonance" with records that they self-consciously created collectibles. "Punk rock gave you the idea of buying things of a series. You could see that labels like Stiff came from a certain design sensibility. New wave was about making collectibles, but a lot of it had to do with your financial stability. I always had to pinch money from my mother's purse before I drove off to New

York. I'd take twenty dollars so I'd have enough money for a Damned album and maybe a sandwich. During the '80s I wound up with so many punk rock singles, ones that would command a couple hundred bucks now. They're the ones that show up on the CD compilations now, and there's nothing like having an original copy, but at the time I had to sell them on St. Mark's Place for cigarette money."

Tours with Sonic Youth have been a more dependable source of fuel for the collection. "It's funny, but a lot of the jazz records I'm looking for are found in Japan. That's the one place on earth that has more highly collectible records than anywhere; it's a collector's dream and nightmare in one dose. You can find whatever you're looking for over there— there are maps, three-hundred-page booklets that list all the record stores in Japan, but you have to decode and decipher them. In Tokyo alone there are one hundred different vinyl stores. Last time I went there I remember looking down from the plane and thinking, 'This is a little island. How can it be such an intensified bastion of record stores?' What I'd do is fill up every corner of my suitcase and my guitar bag; I'd completely line my amp case with records. Then I'd ship a bunch of boxes and get the record label to pay for shipping. I'd say, 'We've got a bunch of Sonic Youth source material here.'"

Perhaps out of sympathy, he hasn't pulled the Stiff trick of making instant collectibles out of his own records. "I don't like to make collectibles, but we've done certain things that are maybe spurred on by the label for business reasons, like 'Europe wants a ten-inch of this single.' And I've done a cou-

ple of things on my own label that came out with five hundred copies and disappeared within a year. But I only do that
because I don't want to wind up with ten thousand copies in
my basement."

Twenty years before punk, ten years before the Beatles, New
York and its record stores had a different rhythm. This time
the music wasn't coming from England, it was coming from
down the street. If you happened to live in New York during
the late '50s, and you were hip enough to be into doo-wop
and other early stirrings of rock 'n' roll, you didn't have to
go to a Montgomery Ward to get the music. You could go
to Times Square and buy it from the source.

One of the city's legendary outlets, The Times Square Record Shop, occupied an underground corner of Canal Street
and Broadway from 1959–62. You'd go there on a Sunday
afternoon, when the middle-aged, bespectacled owner, the
late Irving "Slim" Rose, wasn't busy with his other gig running a jewelry store. The place became a hangout for record
producers and DJs, so it also attracted groups and record
promoters looking for the big break. There might be a few
doo-woppers harmonizing in the corner, and there'd definitely be a few leather-jacketed punks crowding the stairs.
And there'd be Slim cranking the music he loved—usually
the kind of emotive streetcorner soul with a high tenor wailing on top. The store wound up spinning off its own Times
Square label, by some accounts, the first label devoted solely
to doo-wop. It ran from 1960 to 1962, and there are now a

few bootleg compilations devoted to its output.

The scene at Times Square changed a few lives, and Peter Wolf is living proof. Before he came to Boston and wound up touring the world with the J. Geils Band, Wolf was a New York hipster who put in long hours at Times Square as a preteen. "Records became a part of my existence," he recalls. He was barely into adolescence when he heard Elvis Presley's "Heartbreak Hotel" coming from a neighbor's house in the Bronx. "From the window I heard this sound that totally captivated me—'Don't make me so lonely I could die.' My dad was a musician, so records were a part of my world, but at that point it just hit. I walked to the local record store, and the guy told me, 'You're the 20th person that's come in asking for that,' I had to wait until the end of the week before he got it back in."

Weekly trips to Times Square fed his passion. "You'd get off the subway and you'd see all the doo-woppers hanging out there, trading records. You'd see Paul Simon, Dion, all those cats down there. It was Birdland for record collectors, a cultural center, people saying 'I'll give you two of those for one of that.' Something about those labels has a transfixing power for me . . . Gone, End, Chess, Specialty. It was magic. I wound up spending $2.50 for a record, and you just didn't do that. It was one I still have, 'My Heart's Desire' by the Wheels."

Wolf's shadowy figure has become a familiar sight to anyone who frequents nightspots in Boston: he still looks impressively bohemian in his black garb and ever-present shades. He was an all-night disc jockey on Boston's WBCN before he was a rock star, and still draws from the spirit of radio when it was great. On the dedication to his latest album, *Sleepless*, Wolf imagines that broadcast waves are still swirling in space, beaming the voices of Elvis, Hank Williams, and Sam Cooke into the cosmos, creating "an eternal legacy of voices and songs . . . on a sleepless journey." On an afternoon drive through Boston, recently, it seemed his own car radio played nothing but sweet, vintage soul from a few decades earlier. Okay, so it was actually a cassette that a DJ friend had made, but you could be excused for thinking that he'd tapped into those enchanted airwaves.

His Boston apartment looks like a shrine to music fandom. As you walk through the door you find his book collection in the front alcove, and sitting right at eye level is a row of five books sharing one word in the title: "Elvis." However, his most impressive souvenirs are ones that most collectors will never get to see. He shows a postcard that he knows will grab my attention. It was mailed to him in 1968, signed by one Mongo Morrison. He's been hanging out in a "rustic, groovy" part of New York, and wants you to come see him in town next month. A photo of the two together confirms the sender's identity. One-time Boston resident Van Morrison, at that point working on the songs that would become the landmark album *Astral Weeks*. Hell, he may have scribbled the first lyrics to "Madame George" within minutes of writing this postcard. I handle with great care.

His records cover the walls of his main room; nicely organized with the fancy CD boxed sets on an exposed shelf. His huge middle room doesn't have a lot of reclining space, but every corner has something to play music on: a vintage jukebox propped up near the window, a new CD player at the other end, a turntable sitting right on the middle table. Shut away in cabinets just above the floor are the vintage singles, including a few boxes' worth that he's carried around for most of his life. He played them on his radio show (and still does, when he does one of his annual guest broadcasts) and worked up some of the songs with the J. Geils Band, who introduced them to another generation of budding R&B fans. And yes, some of those are the same well-traveled singles he bought on Times Square four decades ago. Wolf's archives are home to some undisputed rock/soul masterpieces. But the disc he's about to play is definitely not one of them.

"Sometimes you find a little oddball record," he notes as he cranks up the turntable, his face showing the hint of a grin. He shows me the 45's sleeve, which lists no artist and gives no info beyond the title: "Stickball—A Bit of Nostalgia." It starts with a heavenly choir, and turns into one of those urban-funk grooves that were all over the radio during the *Shaft* and *Superfly* era. The narrator's got one of those deep-soul voices, doing one of those monologues about how groovy it was to grow up with friends in the projects, "sharing popcorn and grooving with your ice cream." Definitely got some camp value, but so far I have no idea why anyone with a world-class soul collection would be playing me this. "Love between two people is outta sight," notes the narrator. "But love between FIVE people—that's a groove! Especially if I'm one of those five!" The record takes a fast train south from there, as the narrator makes absolutely no bones about what he wants his four partners to do to which parts of him, where and how hard. "The preceding program was brought to you by the makers of Shit," announces the nameless guy over the fadeout, getting in one more offense for the road. Now Wolf is really grinning.

The hell with Woodstock, here's why the late '60s were great. You could hear this thing on a commercial radio station, providing you tuned in during the wee hours. Try a stunt like that nowadays, and your station's corporate office would ride you out of town on a rail. Even Wolf doesn't know who was behind this, which adds to its charm (for the record, you can still find it on a CD compilation called *Naughty Rock 'n' Roll*, where the artist is listed as P-Vert). Wolf says it came out in response to the Beatles's "All You Need is Love," which makes some kind of twisted sense. "The great thing was playing this on the radio. Who'd be listening at 4:30 A.M. except the real congregation?"

That single now resides in one of his stashed-away boxes, along with the other discs that have the longest tenure in his collection. And carrying them around wasn't as easy in the days before CDs. Just imagine a band crowded into a tour bus trying to work a record player. "I used to travel with a phonograph during the days of the J. Geils Band, and a few album boxes. It got a lot easier with the advent of cassettes." Rather than bragging about hits he had with the J. Geils Band, he'll note that he turned other folks on to the R&B that he loves. "That was one of the greatest things about being in the Geils Band. For instance, when I see a Dyke &

the Blazers CD reissue and it's called 'So Sharp' [after a song that the Geils Band covered], I know we helped popularize that group."

Wolf's 45s are clearly records that have been lived with: The discs themselves are in playable shape, but the covers are shot to hell. And the song titles read like messages from another time—like this single by Chuck Higgins, with the song titles printed in bold capitals: On one side, "I NEED YOUR LOVE," on the other, "OH YEAH." "You've gotta know this song," he says handing me a copy of "Love-Itis" by Harvey Scales and the 7 Sounds. In fact, I know it because Wolf's own version was a favorite of mine during high school. His remake is still pretty cool, but it didn't have the brilliant label design of Scales's single: it's on Magic Touch Records, and the label shows a grinning rabbit waving a wand.

There's a visual flair in most of these singles that sets you up for the music; they're already blasting before you start playing them. The original Mercury single of "Tryin' to Get to You" by the Eagles (no, not those Eagles) has a screaming, Day-Glo pink label. For a meaningful, patriotic touch, he pulls out "There's a Star Spangled Banner Waving Some-where," by Elton Britt & the Dominoes—an RCA single with a patriotic red-and-white label. Wolf can hear something in this, but I sure can't: it's a country-ish stinker with a kitschy, dramatic delivery. Then again, it would probably be mistaken for a major statement nowadays. My own idea of a real state-ment is something like the next single I turn up: "That's Where It's At," by an artist listed as "Lots a Poppa— 420 Pounds of TNT." It's on the Tribe label, whose logo is a dimestore-type, politically incorrect Indian in headdress. You don't really have to ask whether the record's any good or not.

Wolf hands over a record with some personal value, explaining that "My first true love found this for me. She rescued it from a barbeque joint that burned down in the Bronx." She couldn't have found a more perfect record: with its deep-blue label and the titles on proud display, this disc already speaks volumes about the pains of young love. It's Little Willie John on the Chess label, with "Do You Love Me"/"Heartbreak (It's Hurtin' Me)."

"Unless they get broken, you never let these things go," he says. For him, the old singles are the quickest route back to the buzz he got in Times Square. He could have found most of these songs on CD reissues, or burned a CD compilation of his own, but it wouldn't be the same. "I get something out of just holding these records," he says. "When I take 'em out, I'm not into putting them back right away. I get into a listening jag with certain things, especially when you get into the bottle and people come by. I love CDs because they preserve the music, but there's a richness and uniqueness that those original records had. So this"—he holds up a select single from the pile—"is the Holy Grail."

It's "Honkin' at Midnight" by Frank Motley & His Motley Crew (no, not that Mötley Crüe), which he pronounces "just a great rock 'n' roll record." What blasts out is a really rude gutteral sax, a rhythm section that's gonna fall over any minute, and a singer barking out a bunch of exhortations: "Come in brother and blow you horn! I wanna honk some mo'!" I can't say whether the thirty-plus years of wear on the grooves has added to the overall effect, but it sure doesn't hurt. "Whoo!" Wolf lets out one of his trademark yelps, getting into the music as if he's onstage. They're supposed to get the pulse racing and the blood level jumping. In this impromptu house party, they've just worked once again.

chapter **II**

MADE IN U.S.A

VJ-CT-III6

LOVE AND VINYL

(B. Milano)

W*ith a* heavy heart, I confront Pat with Robert Crumb's theory that collectors never get lucky. Since Pat's long held a reputation as a ladies' man, I was hoping he could handle the news. "Hell, that's because Crumb only collects 78s," he shoots back with barely a pause. "We all know that 78s aren't sexy. Now, LPs are a different story. Just look at this—" He reaches over to his store's "Living Stereo" section and pulls out an early-'60s bachelor-pad album, *Music to Break Any Mood*, by Dick Schory's Percussion Ensemble, with the requisite cover photo of a hot blonde in jungle garb. "Now, this one will get them going every time."

Okay, so if you're a hopeless collector with a roomful of

records, there's got to be a vinyl aphrodisiac in there some-where. Nobody's ever proved that a complete stock of Julie London or Bryan Ferry albums will help you get any action, but nobody's ever claimed that it hurt. Still, some stereotypes die hard, notably the one that collectors are incapable of sus-taining relationships.

English writer Tanya Headon, in the fanzine *Freaky Trig-ger*, summed up why collectors scare their dates away: "Even the most intimate moments have to have the perfect sound-track, and there's no greater passion-killer than watching your beloved crouching over a multi-CD changer." Nick Hornby's *High Fidelity* did its part to reinforce the theory, suggesting that no woman would bother debating what Elvis Costello's best album is, or bother with a man who did. (A notion that's not entirely true: I can vouch that I once asked a woman out specifically because she knew that the answer, of course, was *Get Happy!!*) At the end of Hornby's book, the hero grows up a little, learns to tone down his passion for vinyl, and recommits himself to his long-suffering, non-collector girlfriend. Some of us thought he should have gone instead with the cool fanzine editor who tried to seduce him with custom mix tapes.

"Who collects records? Mostly people that don't have a dating life," ventures musician Roger Manning. "I've found myself trapped in many obsessive collecting situations that just don't leave room for anything else. I learned to back off, but in my twenties I was pretty wrapped up in it." Engineer Bill Inglot paints an even less flattering picture of those driven to collect. "I know all about those scary record guys, the ones that have 155,000 LPs in their garage—I'm probably in denial because I'm one of them. But I hate to even use the word 'collector.' It implies a guy with taped glasses who can't order food in restaurants."

The mundane truth is that collecting is just one of the many X factors that needs to be negotiated in a relationship, and that it can be a success or a failure like anything else. Manning now has a girlfriend who's more obsessed with obscure psychedelic pop than he ever was. Los Angeles collector and Hollywood Records A&R director Geoffrey Weiss, who stopped counting his collection when it threatened to top one hundred thousand, admits that, "most of my previous girlfriends have laughed at me about it." But he wound up with one who didn't, and he's been married to her for fourteen years.

But train wrecks are always possible as well. As a used-record dealer, Pat has seen a few of those. He recalls being called in to cart away the collection of a musician who had some success as a member of a hit-making late-'60s band. I asked Pat how he could tell that the guy didn't really want to sell his records. "Well, for starters, because he was crying. Meanwhile, his wife kept coming to him and telling him it was the right thing to do. She seemed pleasant enough, but it was obviously her idea. He told me they were both into a religion that involved leaving your body and traveling to other planets, and that earthly possessions like records weighed you down. For him it was like saying goodbye to his youth for the last time. But at least he had the presence of mind to make sure I paid him top dollar.

"I used to have a girlfriend who didn't care for the records," Pat admits. "And she was a music fan, but it got to the
point where she wouldn't go into a record store with me, she
felt it was something that had displaced her. When we dated
for six months and didn't get married, she started saying
things like, 'You ought to just take all those things and throw
them out in the yard.' I told her that there was a greater
likelihood of her being thrown in the front yard than the
records." Not surprisingly, they never got married. "I'm not
saying that I won't start getting rid of my records someday.
But in terms of choosing a suitable relationship, they do have
a way of separating the wheat from the chaff."

There's a time to stick to your guns and a time to recon-
sider, and Steve Turner admits that he caved in just a little.
When he stopped touring on a regular basis with Mudhoney
and money started getting tight, he took his girlfriend's advice
and sold one of his records, and this caused him to re-evaluate
his whole collecting habit. "I unloaded one of my crown jew-
els for a thousand dollars," he says, evincing some obvious
regret. "It was 'Second Generation Rising,' by Jackie Shark
and the Beach Butchers. It's one of those obscure punk singles that everybody wants to track down. Mine was only the
second copy that had ever shown up. Nobody knows where
it came from and it's a great, great record. I wouldn't mind
hearing it now. My girlfriend told me I should sell it, and it
earned me another month of not working. But when I sold
it, that nearly killed my bug for collecting. Psychologically,
I know I'm not that much of a collector if I can sell one of

my prize possessions. If I can get rid of one, then none of them mean as much as I might have thought."

If there are any female collectors out there, we have some bad news to report: Sorry, but you don't exist. At least, that's what a lot of male collectors are convinced. "I'd be interested in finding some, but I've never met a serious woman collector of anything. And I never met a woman record collector at all," says Crumb. To some extent, male record collectors, Crumb included, wear their geekiness as a badge of honor. There's a certain pride that goes along with the self-deprecation. Hell, no woman could possibly be as obsessed as we are. Take away any cheap sexism, and you're left with a more idealized attitude. The idea isn't that women are inferior, but that they've got better things to do. Maybe collectors got warped by the lyrics of too many pop songs, but a lot remain convinced that their habits would preempt their dream girl from coming along.

Even if she does, you're left having to make certain compromises. British comic and novelist Stewart Lee recalls a genuine personal crisis that erupted when he began cohabitating. "I caught myself being truly uncomfortable about the fact that a copy of Queen's album *Live Killers* was going to be coming into my house. I have this notion of myself as a person of taste, and wouldn't want something like that to come in and ruin it. Now, that may not mean anything to anybody but me, but what's in your record collection is a definite statement of self. I could imagine my cool music friends coming around, and thinking that Queen album was something that I bought."

He did relent, however, so this love affair didn't get killed by *Live Killers*. And, he's beaten the stereotype by having his mate's collection and his under the same roof. "My girlfriend understands me pretty well. She says that I go through different phases, like someone might with religious beliefs—you take things to an extreme until you see that they no longer work. And that includes records—you go through a period of listening to all that music, then you come out knowing what the good stuff is and you're fine. I supposed that *High Fidelity* fixed in the public consciousness that a collector is really a sad thing to be. But it doesn't have to be that way."

Toronto director Alan Zweig's independent film, *Vinyl*, was something of a real-life antidote to *High Fidelity*. He profiled a number of Canadian collectors, none of whom were anywhere near as cute as John Cusack, and few of whom seemed destined for a happy romantic ending. (They had some really cool collections, however.) Much of the film concerned the director's own search for the two things he most desired: his perfect soulmate, and a clean copy of *Satan is Real* by the Louvin Brothers. Sadly, he came up empty-handed on both counts. Even though he invested in Joni Mitchell records as a nod to his notion of female taste, he never managed to find the girl of his dreams.

"The problem is, you have to make a decision in your life

to have room for a girlfriend. Collectors have already made a decision not to do that, because the only room they have in their lives is for records," he tells me. "It's not that women don't like it, it's that you're not really in the game. You wake up in the morning and you're thinking about records. Some of the people I know have records lying around everywhere, and if you're with a woman, you're asking a lot for them to get past that. A lot of collectors have found a way to create their own world, they've found a way to make themselves, in quotes, happy. In that way they don't need anybody else."

As his film made abundantly clear, Zweig is definitely the type who wants somebody else, and he admits that things in his life are less bleak than he presented them. "I've had a girlfriend since I did the film, and I may be about to start up with another one. The problem I had with *High Fidelity* is that I couldn't find any collectors who've been through a number of relationships [as the lead character did]. The ones I found were more likely to be married for twenty-five years, to a wife who can at least tolerate their habit. It's usually their high school sweetheart, their first and last girlfriend. I'm not saying it's impossible to be like Cusack, this cool guy who goes through different relationships. But think about it: Have you ever heard about a record collector who left his wife?"

So in Zweig's view, women really have the better deal. Women can be collectors, he says, and they can be music fans. They just can't be geeks. "Even women with lots of records would probably have more emotional attachment to each one of those records than a male collector would have.

Women can love the music and relate to it. But you take a guy that really loves some kind of music, and he's got the potential to look at the back cover and say, 'I wonder what every other record by this guy would sound like? Maybe I can find more records by everybody who played on this one. And maybe I'm gonna start collecting records with guys on the cover who wear red hats, because I like that too.' That's the beginning of obsession, like being into sports and getting into the statistics, and I don't think that women are prone to that."

Pagan Kennedy attributes the gender gap to a simple matter of personal preference. A novelist with a half-dozen published books, she's the type whose mind always seems to be working. Even in a casual talk over coffee she's following diverse ideas, noting the nature of characters that come into the coffeehouse. That kind of creative mind, she suggests, doesn't lend itself to collecting. Women may love music as much as the guys do, but they're less inclined to spend time obsessing over details, especially when it comes to that private ritual of shutting yourself away and communing with your favorite records. "I think a lot of women would find it hard to spend that kind of time alone in a room—I personally would be on the phone after two minutes. That quality of being able to focus all alone—I see more guys who have that quality, which I envy a lot. Because I'd get a lot more work done if I was like that."

Having had two collectors for boyfriends, she's done her best to get into the mindset. "It was hard for me to understand, but I lived with someone that loved collecting books and records—he was more of a stuff-a-holic. I could see that he'd really love something about a cartoon, or a comic book, or the music, and I loved a lot of the same things. But the thing he loved was so ephemeral—it speaks to some feeling, or some world you want to be in, and that's not something you can keep." Her own collecting experience began and ended while researching her book *Platforms*, about '70s pop culture. To properly relive the era, she decided to listen to nothing but 8-track tapes for most of a year. "For starters, it massively limits what you can listen to. It really made me listen to mainstream '70s music, by forcing a selection on me that I would never have been able to pick out if I'd gone looking for it—I hadn't listened to Deep Purple since I was in high school, and I hadn't wanted to either.

"I had friends who collected 8-tracks, and the idea they had was that people who collect them are like the 8-tracks themselves, all warped and broken. I found that very sweet, and the whole idea of collecting hit me the same way."

Not for long, however. "I wound up getting an 8-track carousel that used to be used in bars; you program it the way you program a CD player, but it's analog. And it *so* didn't work. I had a party and decided that the music would only be 8-tracks. I had the worst time at the party, because there was a constant 8-track crisis going on—either 'Pagan, the music stopped!' or 'Pagan, the music sucks!' I spent the whole night nursing the 8-track, and that's when I started turning against it." Thus, her collection of vintage cartridges—a pretty impressive one that she built up during the year she wrote the book—was last seen sitting on the curb outside her apartment waiting for trashpickers.

Miriam Linna, who owns the Norton Records label and is eternally keyed to the primal energy of garage rock and wailing rhythm-and-blues, swears she's never been troubled by any of the above issues. In her world there are simply cool people and uncool people, and a cool person wouldn't let something as important as great records fall by the wayside. Accordingly, she's spent most of her adulthood in a two-collector relationship. She and her husband, Billy Miller, met at a record convention in 1977, when he was running a table and she asked him if he had the killer '60s punk single, "You Must be a Witch" by the Lollipop Shoppe. They played in the Zantees and the A-Bones together, they started the fanzine *Kicks* together, and they currently run the label together. They've also taken the ultimate leap of faith and the true blood-union of a relationship: They've merged their record collections.

"We're probably equally obsessed," she says, "equally convinced in the ultimate greatness of the cool sounds. There are fans of cool music who might go home and the music won't be part of their lives—we're not like that. Our life revolves around what we do, twenty-four hours a day. There's still a stack of records that are unlistened to, there's always stuff to dig up and new things to track down. When we met up and started doing *Kicks* together, we were part of a number of people trying to solve the mysteries that were really important to them—like where a member of some band wound up, or where to find a record that they really dug. We didn't care about converting squares, we just wanted to share it with other people who were into it. At the time, I was really wanting to find more people who dug the Flamin' Groovies. That's how I met Billy and virtually all the people who are still my best friends today."

Even before the couple met up, Linna had been pulled into collecting by her older brother and sister. "They pretty much dictated what was cool, and they were pretty doggone brutal when it came to suggesting anything. For instance, a lot of my best friends at the time were big Monkees fans, but I never was—my sister would have slugged me." Even with their collections merged, she notes that she and her husband have slightly different styles, with him taking a bit of the traditional male role. "I'd say Billy is the world-class collector, he's the one that goes after the heavy-duty rarities, and he's the one who's willing to spend the big bucks. But we combined everything pretty early on. A lot of collectors in couples seem to keep two copies of every record they really care about, but that's not been the case here. The music was the reason we got together, and it's basically what our life has become."

Even in the more traditional realm of collecting—the solitary pursuit, with the records tucked into a private stash—the female collectors are out there. And they've made the same leap of faith—from loving a certain song or band, to wanting all the stuff you can get your hands on, to really needing all that and more—that the guys have. Female collectors are likely to be younger, just as there are more female rock musicians nowadays. The women have been hooked in by different music, and may have different reference points. But that's something that male collectors have to accept: that there may be a few serious collectors out there who care more about the Cocteau Twins than Roky Erikson. They may even own a Queen album or two—but all right, hopefully it's not the live one.

New York publicist Erika Tooker is the type of woman that lonely male collectors are sure they'll never meet—young, sharp and stylish, with a cool music-biz job, and the ability to obsess about records with the best of them. And yes, she's also a geek, if that implies an eye for the piddling details about the records and the endless search for more of the same. I met her at a music conference in Austin, where we talked about a record show that was coming up the next day. She had the outgoing nature of a publicist and the fashion sense of a downtowner, and she'd heard of every obscure band I brought up. I immediately made a mental note to get to the really good tables at the record show before she did.

She's come through a goth phase and a metal phase, not that you'd have a hard time figuring that out (dress: black; hair: black; boots: black). Yet she's never linked up with any of those collector guys. "I've been single for ten years, so where are those people? The weird thing is that I meet tons of guys like me, hardcore record collectors, but since I'm just like them, they want to be my buddy—they'd rather have some bimbo for their girlfriend. If a boy comes over and I want to wow him with my collection, I can always pull out my Stones record—*Their Satanic Majesties Request*, with the original 3D cover." Maybe the problem is that she's gone to record shows with her male friends, and grabbed the choice items before they did. "Yeah, I'm one of those people—if I walk into a record shop with someone, hell hath no fury. When I spot something I want, get out of the way, it's mine."

"I would agree that record collecting is a male thing," she says. "But I'm into the full-on geekery, I have to have the right record in perfect condition. When I was a kid, none of my friends collected records, and the ones that did were guys. All my girlfriends were into how cute the guys in the bands were, instead of the music—which moved me more than the bands' looks." Otherwise, her reference points were pretty much the same as those of most other collectors. Her father also had the fever; his thing was baseball memorabilia and he had an autographed ball from Mickey Mantle. "I've been a collector at heart since I was young. There's always been something—I still have my Smurf glasses from when I was ten. I've found that the airport makes it easy for collectors: you've got shot glasses, snow globes and magnets. I went for the shot glasses because I love to drink. And now the record shop is the first place I ever go when I travel."

Now in her early 30s, Tooker grew up in a different culture than her collecting bretheren—no Elvis (Presley), Beatles, or (early) Rolling Stones on the radio for her—but it was a pivotal moment when the impulse took hold. "I used to have a record player with the entire cast of *Welcome Back, Kotter* on the front. My first record came from my parents. I was probably seven years old. They bought me *Physical* by Olivia Newton-John. I listened to it all of three times, and then I stole my brother's Kiss records. *Rock and Roll Over*—now that is a fucking great record.

"From there I didn't want my brother's collection, I wanted my own. I got to love the physical act of buying a record, when you're carrying it under your arm and people think you're the coolest person on earth; you just bought a record!" As a teen she hung out at Bleecker Bob's, the same Greenwich Village store where Thurston Moore put in plenty of quality time—though Erika staked out her own territory in the metal section. "Hanoi Rocks, Faster Pussycat, all that crap. A lot of my collection probably means more to me than anybody else. Like my Sisters of Mercy seven-inches— you can't even sell those on eBay now. But I met [singer] Andrew Eldritch and had him sign one, like the little loser I am. He was pretty grumpy, but it worked out—I gave him a cigarette, he signed my record."

Erika's life proves that some things are universal: no matter your gender or the era in which you started collecting, you still grow up thinking that there are tiny people inside the radio singing, and that the people who work at record stores are the coolest on the face of the earth. ("Record Stop on Long Island. With all the import picture discs hanging up in a row—I still have all their shelves in my imagination.") And that the very existence of certain records is enough to send you on a quest that could last years. And especially that the chase is better than the catch.

"The one that did it for me was an instrumental remix of 'Unfinished Sympathy' by Massive Attack, a different version than any of the usual ones. The DJ played it during a Catherine Wheel show at Irving Plaza, and I thought it was the greatest thing I'd ever heard. I couldn't get through to the DJ to ask about it, maybe I was buzzed and I didn't care. Finally found it in a record store on Barrack Street, after a search of six or seven years. I immediately started making these high-pitched squeals, feeling like a total loser. Then I took it home, played it ten times in a row, and probably never listened to it again. But it's the thrill of the chase."

There is one romantic tragedy for collectors, and Erika experienced it when her last relationship broke up. Never mind that they can break your heart, what's worse is that they can steal your records as well. "I have thousands of CDs, and I could tell which particular ones were missing. And I could feel the steam rising out of my ears." Though we never dated, I assured her that I would never pull such a dirty trick. I'm too much of a gentleman, with too strong a code of honor. And besides, I always hated the Sisters of Mercy.

*T*here are domestic records, and there are imported records—except in England, where it's the other way around (thank you, Bob & Doug McKenzie). Many of us who grew up as Beatles nuts remember those magic words that were in the upper-right-hand corner of every Beatles record: "Recorded in England."

The Beatles turned me into a record geek, and they've reminded me over the years that I still am one. This became glaringly apparent when I went to my first and only Beatles convention in the early '90s. I wasn't there just to spend money or to gawk at pristine "butcher" covers and old Apple labels: I wanted to hang out with the truly diehard, to see those who were more devoted than I'll ever be. The two friends I'd come with had similar agendas. Andrew was barely into his 20s and already an authority on '60s pop; David was a musician who could play obscure Kinks and Beach Boys songs note-for-note. But we all prided ourselves on having things in proper perspective, never having gone too far over the top.

Here was where we were sure we'd find the people whose addiction would put ours to shame. People staring longingly at those scratched-up '60s singles and beating a path for the bank machines? Too far gone, we thought smugly. We even saw a few people staring devotedly at four anonymous guys playing in a Beatles tribute band the way kids might look at one of their dad's friends who turns up in a store wearing a Santa Claus suit. "Get a life," we sneered under our breath, as somebody made off with the rare 1965 fan magazine that we'd come this close to getting for ourselves.

The real attraction for us was a question-and-answer session with Harry Nilsson, the legendary songwriter who was a favorite of the Beatles, a drinking partner of John Lennon's, and the writer of many cult hits. Sadly, this turned out to be his last public appearance before his death in 1993. He looked heavier than we remembered, but it was enough to hear traces of Nilsson's singing voice when he answered a question. He was a notoriously stage-frightened performer, and he never gave a full concert. Most of the questions concerned his drinking days during Lennon's "lost weekend," but we were more interested in asking about the stories behind some early, pre-stardom singles he'd made that we were always fond of. "God knows," he responded. "I was probably just trying to get on the hit parade." Yes, it seemed we were more interested in this particular artist's music than the artist himself.

Our last stop was a Beatles trivia contest, which we thought would provide another opportunity to sneer at the truly devoted. But we were surprised at how easy the questions were, and more astounded that none of these other die-hards knew the answers. The chart single released by a Beatle without the rest of the band? Well, that would be the Plastic Ono Band's "Give Peace a Chance" . . . but everybody knew that, right? Song originally known as "Scrambled Eggs"? That, of course, was "Yesterday" . . . grade-school stuff, for sure. We were now beginning to get admiring looks from the shady folks in Beatles wigs that we'd been chuckling at.

At least we felt sure we'd be eliminated by the tiebreaker question: Name three Beatles's songs that include a count from one to four. The first was easy: everybody knows that count of "One-two-three-FAH!" that begins "I Saw Her Standing There," one of Paul's most manic moments. For some reason the second popped into my mind as well: the count from one to seven, followed by "All good children go to heaven"—the lovely and spooky outro to "You Never Give Me Your Money." But we were stuck for the third, and I absently muttered "One, two, three, four . . ." ". . . Can I have a little more," chimed in Dave. Of course: the counting lyric of "All Together Now." Much to our embarrassment, we won. And we made our way sheepishly to the front of the room to pick up our prizes: color posters of original album covers.

Obviously in disgrace, we made our way to the exit door, all the while getting besieged by folks who acted as though we were surrogate Beatles ourselves. "So have you ever heard the Electric Oz Band single that John produced?" asked a gentleman in horn-rim glasses. "Never heard of it!" I stammered on the way out. (The correct answer would have been, "uh, yes.") "Look, we're all normal!" David said, just out of earshot. "We all have jobs, and we've all had relationships with women!" It was no avail: we were exposed as the biggest Beatles nerds in greater Los Angeles—for that weekend, anyhow.

September 1975. I'm three months out of high school, hitting London on a study-abroad program. For the first time in my life, I can do anything I please. My parents are a continent away, and nobody can stop me from seeking out sex, drugs or whatever I please. I've just turned eighteen and I'm totally free. I figure it took me forty-five minutes to find a good record store.

Beginning with my preteen Beatles fixation, I'd long assumed that the records that came from England were the most exotic ones. At home in the States, you could only get them from stores that were hip enough to have an "import" section, they had sleeker covers, thick plastic bags, and sold for a buck more than regular discs (this would have been a whopping $5.50 in those days). Before punk rock reared its head, the import bin was full of art-rock weirdness—Tangerine Dream, Mike Oldfield, Guru Guru, and Nektar, all with the obligatory sci-fi conceptual covers. You didn't even need to hear the things—and I still haven't heard a note of Guru Guru— just browsing them was an adventure. Was there really a country full of people who listened to this stuff? The twin offensives of synth-pop and MTV cured some of my Anglo- philic tendencies in later years, but I'll still seek out anything Paul Weller, Robyn Hitchcock or Andy Partridge had the slightest thing to do with.

I recall the first record I saw that came from another coun- try. In sixth grade a classmate had the Canadian version of "One" by Three Dog Night. For starters, it was more exotic because it was on RCA—and not even the standard RCA label, but a bright red variation that had the dog along the side instead of on top—rather than the pale-gray Dunhill label everybody else had. When I played it, I had another surprise. Instead of fading out like it did on the radio, it came to a cold ending with a long, sustained chord. (In retrospect, big deal: The Canadians had just used the slightly longer album version instead of the standard single version.) When I told my classmates about my amazing discovery, the universal, across-the-board response was "Huh?"—and I have yet to see any of them at record shows. For myself, I'd found the thrill of having something, even just a minor variation, that every- body else ain't got.

The English record bins were full of items like that. I made my way to a store in Soho, making a point to find a store in Brighton just so I could quote the obvious Who line (though, after all this time, I haven't got the heart). Whoever ran the store was playing an album by a folksinger with a distinctively weird howl in his voice (one of the earlier, less polished, Roy Harper albums), and the records in the bins were even more exotic than the imports at home. I'd heard "Autobahn" on the radio the previous summer, but who knew there existed a whole section of Kraftwerk albums? Or obscure art-rock bands named after Shakespeare's heroines? (There must be one or two Cressida fans out there somewhere?) The records I found on my first U.K. trip remain some of my most prized possessions—not so much the Pink Floyd singles that I've long been sick of, but more outre finds like "Make a Daft Noise for Christmas" by the Goodies, a ridiculous holiday single that I scored at Woolworth's in Inverness, Scotland, and am proud to stick on party tapes to this day. Sure, Elton John's "Island Girl" was a hit then, too, but it's been heard too many times to evoke anything. Cressida or the Goodies will always sound like England in 1975.

Even though the oddball records will always conjure England for me, I couldn't find anyone in England who actually listened to them, except for one ethereal girl who said she went home and studied to Tangerine Dream—obviously someone after my own heart. Most of my U.K. classmates listened to the same commercial hits that everyone played in America. I would have loved to find out who my U.K. counterparts were, who were scouring the bins for those weird psychedelic records. And I've got one answer: Nick Salamon was.

Salamon is an automatic friend to anyone who's drooled over eccentric British psychedelic records. As the one-man-band Bevis Frond, he's made many such records himself, and he can do the music-geek thing with the best. Small example: on the just-released CD reissue of the early Bevis Frond album *Triptych*, there is a track that was never released the first time around—because, the notes say, it was too obviously a Caravan ripoff. (Prog-rock again: Caravan made one of the great lost art-rock albums, *In the Land of Grey & Pink*.) And that's part of his worldview in a nutshell: not only would he venture to rip off Caravan, he'd assume that significant numbers of people would notice if he did.

So far he's managed to enjoy a stable domestic life, despite the fact that he owns four copies of the first Mad River album. He may not be a '60s relic, but that album certainly is. Mad River was a psychedelic San Francisco band that was darker and doomier than the rest, and their album had a twelve-minute song, "The War Goes On," that probably caused its share of freakouts at the time. It couldn't have sold more than a couple thousand copies and, to repeat, Salamon owns four of them. "You ought to see Nick Salamon's house," says friend and occasional collaborator Stewart Lee, a novelist and stand-up comic. "It's like a storage facility in there."

"God, it's tragic, but I do have my moments of complete nerdism," Salamon says. "I bought Mad River when it first came out, and then I found a copy in much nicer condition than mine—but I had to keep my original because it was the first copy I owned, and it's got my name written on it. So that's two copies on vinyl. Then I had to get the first CD on Edsel, because it was mastered at the right speed—the vinyl was mastered at the wrong speed, so their CD was slowed down to correct it. But that didn't sound right, because I'd been hearing it at the wrong speed since 1968, so I had to buy another CD with the fast version.

"So now I'm here with four copies, when I know that one would have sufficed. And I'm there saying, 'Why am I buying this? I've already got it!' But I know I'm just a mark punter and I don't really care," he says, his English colloquialisms coming out as he shows his true colors. "I know that as soon as they invent another format, I'll go out and buy another copy of the first H.P. Lovecraft record—there's another one that I have three copies of, because the first CD was mastered off a not-very-good condition record. But it drags on, doesn't it? I've sold a lot of records, but the only ones I could bear to part with are the ones I didn't really like in the first place. If I do like it, I'll keep buying it again. So, yeah, I'll be there in ten years buying a surround audio DVD of *Savage Resurrection*." (Another obscure cult classic of psychedelia; from a California band whose one album includes a thing in E titled, uh, "Thing in E".)

The people who've met Salamon over the years aren't exactly shocked to find out that he's a record collector, especially if they already know he's a musician. "New acquaintances might be a bit taken aback to see my collection. But because I have longish hair and don't have a regular job, I'm seen as the old hippie geek anyhow. So it's expected that I should have a pile of tatty vinyl." This he does—about six thousand albums and singles, some of which he purchased as long ago as 1968. And if that's a relatively small collection, keep in mind that he's absorbed and gotten rid of a few times that number over the years.

If a fire were to hit his house, he insists that he wouldn't immediately start saving records. He's got a wife, kid and a couple of cats who get priority. After that, however, the vintage 45s would likely be the next thing to be rescued. "Those British psychedelic singles are my favorites, and they're really hard to find now. And it has to be the originals instead of the reissues because . . . Oh God, because they're nicer. They're the real thing, and that means there's something special about them. The point is that when they were put out, they weren't released as collectible artifacts. They were released as a current band doing what it did, and putting its single in the shop. People would say, 'Oh, I'll buy that single, Dad,' and they'd take the little record home and put it on their little turntable. For the band it was, 'Look, this is what we do, here it is.' I like that they were done with that in mind, not with any thought of the collector value. If you find it on a reissue, it comes in a package with a lot of words, some bogus description of how it will blow your mind. Not that I don't like a nice archival thing, but it just wasn't done for the same reason as the original—it's not a band putting forward its work, it's a company finding a niche in the market. So you might as well be asking why someone would want an original painting and not a print. It looks the same, but it ain't the same."

This outburst comes after he's spent most of an hour insisting that he doesn't really collect. But we've touched a nerve, and the truth comes out. "You regulate what you take in. It's like drinking too much—I do like a drink now and then, but I don't get pissed all the time. Same way with music: I listen all the time but I don't sit there with my eyes spinning, having had an overdose of Ultimate Spinach." (Hippie-ish band from Boston, made three albums that were truly over-the-top, achieving a lysergic silliness that would be well-nigh impossible today, at least without irony. To find out if you're truly into this kind of music, their "Ballad of the Hip Death Goddess" would make a fine acid test, pun intended.) "Their first two albums were really good in a cheesy kind of way," he says, detecting a bit of disbelief from his interviewer.

Salamon's the first to admit that fans of his own music probably share his mindset. No slouch as a songwriter or gui-tarist, he's one of indie rock's most prolific figures. Most Bevis Frond albums are eighty-minute epics, often done with no-body else's help. In the youth and fashion-obsessed world of modern rock, he's an anomaly. Having rounded fifty and never lost his fascination with '60s music, he's seen less as a throwback than as a genuine psychedelic figure of the present day. Though he can write a spiffy pop song when the mood strikes, the real payoff of a Bevis Frond show comes when he dashes one of his trademark ten-minute guitar solos, let-ting the spirit of those long-forgotten '60s bands come out to play.

Being an artist and a collector have gone hand in hand, since he picked up a guitar as a preteen and gave his grade-school audience a version of Brian Hyland's "Ginny Come Lately"—a song that was never a mainstream hit in any country. "Creating music and listening to it, to me they're not different things, and one doesn't get in the way of the other. Every time I hear something I like I go off and write my own version of it, which I hope winds up sounding like me. For me it's like relaxation. I come home, put my feet up and write a song. I could write three songs a day for the rest of my life, and I probably will."

He's also an anomaly among record collectors, since he's apparently never sacrificed anything—other than a few quid for Mad River reissues—to feed his lifestyle. He hasn't had to worry about carting his collection around, since he's had the same London residence for the past twenty-two years. He's had the same best friends for even longer: he and two friends still have pieces of a record collection that they pooled in the '6os. "There was my mate Kevin and my mate Mick, two guys I'm still in touch with; in fact, I just went to Kev's fiftieth birthday party. In the '6os we used to pool our money together every week, buy an album between us, then go round to somebody's house and decide who wanted what. That way we could pool ten shillings each and have something new every week from a store in Church Street Market where albums cost one pound ten shillings."

While he's acquired and shed a few collections since then, those formative purchases remain prized possessions. "I started buying records in 1958, when I was five. I grew up in the center of London, where there were always stores that sold televisions and radios, then you'd go to the back of the shop where the record collection was. I was nine when the Beatles came out, but before that I was buying American stuff—the Chantays, the Surfaris, the Crickets. All the stuff

that was really influential when I started, I've never gotten
rid of. That Johnny Duncan & the Bluegrass Boys EP I
bought in 1958—still got that. And my copy of *With the Beatles*, the one with my name written in a childish hand on the
back. Those are the important artifacts, because it's the same
for all of us—those were the really formative years. You're a
teenager, you're growing up, so those are more than just
ephemeral things. And I can still play all of mine, because
I'm a bit of an archivist. I grew up with my mum and I knew
I had to take care of my stuff, because if I lost it I'd never
have it again."

My real discovery, however, is that he could well have
been the guy servicing those remote English record bins that
I used to browse. Before he began making records, he worked
as a dealer. And being just a little obsessed meant that he
could sell choice items to people who were a whole lot obsessed. "I didn't like my job and I did like records, so I made
a point of combining the two. I went to a few record conventions and was looking at the prices, thinking, 'Jesus, I can
pick this stuff up for next to nothing.' If you've been buying
records all your life, you tend to know what's sought after
and what isn't. I specialized in psychedelia, which was what
I was fondest of and what I knew the most about. If you've
been into something for the best part of your life, you tend
to know a bit about it. And in the early '80s that was pretty
much an untapped area. Everybody was into rock 'n' roll and
punk, but nobody was touching psychedelic or progressive
rock. So I could buy albums with a Vertigo swirl [the dizzying
design on a fondly-remembered '70s label] for a quid and sell

them off for seven. I'd go around to all the shops I knew in southeast England—Friday I'd be in Nottingham and Saturday I'd be in Southampton. Much to my amazement I made about three times as much selling records as I could working. Halcyon days, mate."

Only trouble was that he wound up taking home nearly as many discs as he sold. "You know how it is—you see a nice record going for a pound and you think, 'Oh, that's nice. I'll take that.' So I went through a period of getting everything, but I was always torn. After six months I'd realize that I didn't like something that much after all. You start to wonder if you really need an album by the Bakerloo Blues Line [a British R&B band who never caught on]. So I wound up cutting my collection down pretty drastically. But let's face it, records and music have been with me since I was a little boy, and they'll be with me when I'm an old man."

Did we just hear him say he wasn't a real collector? Well, up to a point. "I've always felt there's more to life than records. I do love them, but I like other things in life as well. I think there are people who are into music above anything else, and I think they need to get out more."

Or maybe we can just visit our friends' houses, because sometimes it seems that there's only one record collection, and everyone who collects winds up sharing the same items. Case in point: Stewart Lee is a good ten years younger, and doesn't make his living in the music business. He didn't start collecting until the '80s, and it was new wave and ska singles that initially looped him in. Two-Tone records was going strong at the time, so Lee was buying those Specials and

Selecter singles when he was ten. So he grew up in a slightly different era with different reference points—but you visit his house and you'll still find some of the same psychedelic/art-rock records that I used to chase down, for all I know, maybe some of the same copies. Just goes to show, that sometimes all roads lead to Faust. Or to the West Coast Pop Art Experimental Band, a late-'60s outfit beloved by a majority of diehard collectors, and by hardly anybody else.

"There's got to be a shared sensibility among people who are curious, that you find that the same things are valuable," he notes. "You listen to that much music, you ultimately reach the point where you know what the good stuff is. Someone who collects records all their lives will end up being a Bob Dylan fan—I mean, there's something objectively great about Bob Dylan, and it always comes down to that." But the West Coast Pop Art Experimental Band? "The point with that is, it was the first psychedelic record I ever heard—'The Spell of Incense.' Andy Kershaw played it on the radio in 1983. That got me into '60s music, one of the ultimate destinations of the record collector. Only trouble was that when the single finally turned up, it was only two minutes thirty seconds, edited down from the six glorious minutes on the album. I could spend a lifetime hunting that kind of thing, and I don't care if it's the original single or a reissue—long as I get to hear it."

Only trouble is that you can't be rational and still be a collector. Look hard enough at your own collection and you're guaranteed to find some things that nobody in their right mind would own. Lee himself gets hit by this revelation as we're talking. "Do I really need a boxed set of Pete Seeger's American folk songs for children? You can hang on to things for sentimental value, but I'm here looking at things that I didn't even like fifteen years ago. The worst part is that there's really a notion here that you're putting on some kind of display of your good taste: Look at me, I'm a bit eccentric! I have Pete Seeger's folk songs, and you can't pin me down! I've seen what happens when collectors go around to each other's houses, and there's a territorial sizing up. Okay, so I'm staring at my collection and I see the last Quicksilver Messenger Service album. Why have I got that? It's really bad."

Indeed, that Quicksilver album—made when the core members of the band had largely scattered—is probably a blot on an otherwise solid collection. It's definitely too bad that Lee's wife couldn't have brought in a record of real depth and quality—something like "Make a Daft Noise for Christmas."

CHAPTER

13

SIDE B
33⅓

EXTREME COLLECTING

I *get* a phone call
from Pat, who tells
me to come down to the record store right away, Jerry the
DJ is hanging out there today. "You want to meet a truly
obsessed collector, you have to see this one." "Get here
quick," says a co-worker out of earshot. "You think it's easy
keeping an eye on this guy?"

I'd long known Jerry by reputation, and had once wit-
nessed one of his famous performances in the subway. He'd
be there on the train platform with his console and his headphones, manipulating the turntables and inciting the crowd
to dance, shouting innuendo in a tone somewhere between
Little Richard and RuPaul—"Do me baby, yeah! Whooo!"—
in short, a classic-model disco DJ out of the *Thank God*

It's Friday realm. The only problem was that the turntables weren't plugged into anything, and there weren't any records on them. The party was entirely in Jerry's head.

Local record-store owners are well familiar with Jerry's act. Despite what he admits is a longstanding "stealing problem," he's managed to work at nearly every used record store in town—not just because the owners have a real affection for him, but because a truly knowledgeable disco enthusiast is hard to come by in such a rock-obsessed city. One store went so far as to install a "Jerry baffle," a wood obstacle designed to foil his habit of sneaking choice records through the counter and into his carrier bag. His friends in record stores also keep him from letting his record-buying habit throw him into debt. If he can bring in a receipt that shows he's paid his phone and electric bills, they'll let him shop for vinyl. By this system, Jerry's bought up all the old disco records that more trend-conscious collectors have thrown into the bins, along with the disco spinoffs—techno, trance, house—that have come along since then.

His other community of choice, the gay community, has likewise come to appreciate Jerry's eccentricity. During Boston's annual Pride Parade, he hooks up his own float with a customized sound system, blaring one of his homemade disco mixes, attaches a rope and hauls it down the street. Considered an odd curiosity at first, this is now regarded as a time-honored tradition, though he says that "I had to give up doing the float a couple of years ago because I was building it in my apartment and it was a fire safety hazard." He's performed a similar act for Red Sox fans on the street before baseball games, though with a far less friendly audience. We can safely assume that Jerry's hulking build has kept him out of big trouble more than once.

The first impression you'd get of Jerry would be that he'd make a good football player, except in this case the player would have to be Dennis Rodman (that gets confirmed by the dye in Jerry's hair, neon blonde on the occasion I met him), but even Rodman probably wouldn't be seen carting around the oversized stereo headphones that Jerry sports at all times and the 1979 Technics turntable that's slung under his arm. "I hear you're world-class," I say by way of greeting. "Yeah, and I have a lot of records, too," he replies.

Jerry's low-grade mental illness finds one outlet in his highly developed grasp of details. Not only can he reel off minutiae about the last thirty years of dance music and the model variations of his beloved Technics turntables, he also knows endless trivia about trains and roller coasters. He hasn't always been able to handle his bills or hold a job, and the Department of Social Services currently pays for the house where he stashes thousands of vinyl finds. But though it hasn't always been that way, his DJ life is partly for real. He's started putting his mixes on homemade CDs and selling them for ten bucks, working the local stores enough to sell a few dozen copies of each. After years of mixing in his living room pretending to DJ for an audience, he's started actually working a few dance clubs, his street profile at least giving him some brand-name recognition. Thus those headphones of Jerry's are more than an escape mechanism, they're the cord that wires him to the outside world.

"This one is only 109 beats per minute," he points out, referring to the Bob Marley track that's playing in the background of the pizzeria where we've stopped for a slice. "I could play this on the subway when I'm out there making people enjoy themselves and have fun. See, these headphones I'm wearing are so powerful that when I'm playing on the subway, the music goes out the other end and people start dancing to it." With that Pat's eyes shoot up across the table. Nope, a pair of headphones with that much power hasn't been invented just yet. "What do we call that, Jerry?" "It's a big fat DJ lie," he responds, grinning like a kid who's been caught making up stories.

Jerry wears an old Stanton 680 phonograph cartridge as a medallion around his neck, and also brings a bag full of LPs with him—as it turns out, a bag that he keeps sealed up and totes as a prop. Lately, he's been buying up turntables at yard sales, even though they're long past working. "I just use them to collect as relics from the '70s," he explains. But when I ask why he bothers carrying a turntable that won't play, he appears flustered for a moment—and I'm nervous that I may have just upset some of his balance—but Jerry rebounds nicely. "I know it's kind of silly, but it's something I like to do. It's the way I display myself as a representative of music." Come to think of it, I wore my Ramones T-shirt to the store for pretty much the same reason.

Jerry's conversation is peppered with reminiscences about his life—when he was four, he was photographed with a 45 rpm record in his mouth—and musical reflections. Silver Convention's "Fly Robin Fly" was the record that set him on his way. Now he'll listen to anything but current rap, which he deems too violent. He claims he's about to hit New York to spin at a club before Pat gives him the look. "No, I'm really just going down there to promote my existence." I ask if his dream is to be a full-time DJ and he responds that no, his biggest dream is to be Diana Ross lying on a beach. "Get down that I'm also a creator of homemade boom boxes," he says when he sees me writing. "I can hook together nine boom-boxes so the sound is monstrous."

I glance over at Pat, thinking I've caught Jerry in another lie. But no, that one was for real. He's good with sound systems, as Pat found out years ago on his first trip to Jerry's apartment. Not only did Jerry mix for hours, he drew a giant Pac-Man on the wall to make it look more like a club. And at the end of the night, he made sure to tell his two guests to drive safely on the way home.

A rock musician himself, Pat has a high tolerance for personal quirks, and the fatherly tone he takes with Jerry is tinged with real admiration. "For a long time all of the gigs he worked were just big DJ lies, but they became real, didn't they?" Jerry nods. "I saw him dancing on the street by Copley Square, carrying on like you never did see. His hair was purple, and he was like a burning flame." Jerry nods quietly, like any performer having his ego stroked offstage. He says, "I was doing that before Rodman ever happened." It was partly through Pat's prodding that Jerry got his chance to play for a real audience. "You have to start by pretending, that's the way everybody becomes everything. Jerry is totally without pretense, and that's what sets him apart from other record collectors who'll build a myth around how interesting their lives are." In other words, a lot of collectors will lie about themselves. Jerry just lies about everything else.

Back in the store, Jerry's put on one of his mix discs, and it's a good one, modern house music with the hummable hooks of classic disco. And when he tells me where and how he devised each segue, it's clearly too detailed to be one of his big fat DJ lies. Eccentric or not, the guy knows his stuff, and I fork over money for a mix. "So I bet you didn't know I really had skills," he says in what seems an unguarded moment. "We always knew you had skills, Jerry," says the young girl behind the counter. Knowing he's got an audience, he sets up his turntables—easy enough, since he still doesn't bother plugging them in—and starts exhorting people to dance, punctuating the songs with "whoos!" and miming to turntable segues like a kid with an air-guitar—except that these segues really were his, back in his apartment. He's in a netherworld where fantasy and reality are mixed up and blurred. But isn't that where disco came from in the first place?

The Velvet Underground famously sang about a girl whose life was saved by rock and roll—in Jerry's case, it's more like his sanity was saved by disco. For many collectors, it works in just the opposite way. Their real lives are perfectly normal, with careers and families and the rest. It's only through their collecting that a more eccentric side of their personalities will emerge.

———

Jim Lahatt is the live music coordinator for BBC's Radio Two, a man that thousands of musicians from both sides of the Atlantic have worked with. He has a life that most music-heads would envy—not just for his job, but for the fact that he's got Paul McCartney's home phone number, and that Brit-pop legends Paul Weller and Oasis members Noel and Liam Gallagher are among his friends. He's very much a professional and, as someone with an encyclopedic knowledge of music and an unquenchable love for it, he's the type of personality that's in short supply on American radio. Someone in his position wouldn't necessarily need to even buy records, since his work would bring him more than enough freebies to bring home at the end of every workday. Yet Lahatt may well be the most obsessive record collector in this book, if not the world.

"You always get the buzz, to begin with, every time you walk into a good store," he tells me. "It's really like a drug fix. You always walk into the store with that feeling of 'I'm going to hit the jackpot;' if that doesn't happen you're depressed until you hit the next shop. And I'm telling you the whole truth. When I walk into a record store, I, personally, get so excited that I have to run to the bathroom. And it isn't number one, mate. I'm talking number two."

It's easy to find good arguments why you're not a total record geek, especially if you really are one. Maybe you think you haven't got the disease because you truly, honestly, plan to listen to all twenty thousand of the albums you own on a regular basis. Or because you don't have the same musical tastes as the collectors you know (this is a good defense, since collecting and music snobbery go hand in hand). Or because you just went out on a date and realized you were normal after all. Maybe you can point to some friend who's far more obsessed than you are: talk to my crazy friend who owns six copies of the first 13th Floor Elevators album, instead of the mere five that I've got.

But someone like Lahatt belongs to the realm of the truly intrepid collectors, where such arguments just don't apply. In the end it's not about cash laid out, but devotion—how much of your time, your sanity, and your personal space you're willing to part with. For the most devoted, record collecting becomes a physical, even psychedelic experience—as Lahatt's bathroom confession well illustrates.

"It's an obsession, and everybody who's into this is obsessed in a different way," he says. "There's nobody at the top. The longer you've been doing this, the more records you're going to have. You just need to buy vinyl, it's truly never ending. I've never met anybody in this league who recovers." Seven-inch singles are Lahatt's drug of choice, and so far he's managed to cram a good fifty thousand of them into a two-bedroom flat in central London. "Property in London is not cheap, and you can't move in my guest room for all the records. If I want another place I'm going to need half a million pounds, but I'm still collecting. I'm married, and I never go on vacation except to places with record shops—no holidays in the sun for me. We went to Turkey on our honeymoon and that was the worst time of my life. Aside from bootleg cassettes, you can't find anything there."

His musical roots are fairly standard ones. Initially raised on classical, he pricked up his ears when BBC DJ John Peel started playing punk rock. This interest led to Mod revivalism, which led to '60s soul and garage rock. But the peculiar passion for the records themselves was something that hit him from the get-go.

"I think the moment I first bought vinyl, I felt it: the quality of the sleeve, the texture, the smell, I just felt everything." His collection grew through his early years as a punk fan and club DJ, and he reckons that it currently grows at the rate of about two thousand pounds per month. Access to eBay and other online sites has made it possible for him to go trawling for records on a daily basis, which he gladly does. "To me life is working all day and coming home and doing my Internet. If a collector has something especially good I'll go see him. All the money I have has always gone into records; if I had a thousand pounds when I was 16 I would have spent it all then. I have more now, so I put more into it."

And no excuses: If you love a record, you need the original pressing. He's developed his own aesthetic about collecting, having earned the right to a bit of snobbery. "I wouldn't call it collecting to buy new releases, you only have to go down to the shop to do that. And I don't go to record shows, I figure that the dealers have had their pick before you even get there."

For him, the experience of finding a new store and unearthing a rare treasure is more than enough to make up for the missed beach days. And by now he's an expert on where those stores are. "New York is one of the worst cities I've ever encountered for record collecting. Absolutely bugger-all, and some of the rudest people in the States as well. But I've found great stuff in places like Burlington, Vermont. There was a small store there that had a lot of great punk and power pop. If you walk into a store and you see masses and masses of records, you just start getting high. If the collection is all in cardboard boxes under the desk, you know you're going to find something. The best time I've had lately was in a shop in Mill Valley, outside of San Francisco. It was a small shop that specialized in jazz and country, and I asked if he had any singles. What he had was a batch that went from floor to ceiling. I knew it was there, but I didn't see anything straightaway. So I warned my wife, and that store took up four days of a ten-day holiday."

He knew he was onto something when his first pass through the boxes turned up original singles by the '60s psychedelic bands, the Spades and the 13th Floor Elevators. "I picked up a few, brought them to the counter, and he said, 'Those are three for a dollar.' So I said, 'Right, I'll take all of them.' That's what gets me excited. It's one thing to find something on eBay, but when you get something for a bargain price; that's really the best."

Thus, the famous names on his Rolodex matter less than a shot at finding a rare single by some unknown and long-defunct band. "I'm not a personality fan; I care about the music. I wouldn't want to meet somebody like [psychedelic eccentrics] Roky Erickson or Sky Saxon, because you hear stories about them, and I don't want any autographs, because I'd rather have the album mint, without the guy signing it.

The bands I collect are the kind who released one single and disappeared, and a lot of times you wind up buying the single from those people anyway, because they sell their own records on eBay. If they're nice people when you meet them it's great; if they're complete and utter dickheads it's bad—but it's the records that I'm after. That's why I get on with people like the Oasis boys, because they're normal people. And a lot of them will come to me with things they're looking for. Graham Coxon (Blur guitarist) was trying to find a copy of the album *Lithium* by Samhain [an early death-metal cult item], and I helped him get it for a reasonable price."

The records have taken a toll on his mobility, and might have done the same to his marriage if his wife didn't understand. "Obviously, space in the house is a problem. The spare bedroom is long gone, but there used to be a little space in front of the turntable. Now that's gone as well. I spend something like two thousand pounds a month. In terms of traveling, I've been to New York, San Francisco, L.A., Seattle, Portland, New England. I'd love to go to Texas, but my wife doesn't like the South. She used to come into record stores with me, but now she'll walk around and see the sights, and we'll meet at some appointed time, which I always go over. She really wants to go to the Bahamas, but the problem is that sunny weather is not really associated with records. And I'm not into reggae or ska."

But even he insists that he's not the most obsessed collector around, though the even harder-core ones may well be urban legends. He says, however, that he's heard of people who'll buy every available copy of certain rare singles, rather than settling for one. And, he insists, there are poor souls who'll literally buy anything, and at least he's ruled by musical taste. "Every time I start filing alphabetically, there are another two-hundred singles to be filed. There's no point, it's never ending. I've bought some things to trade them later, but when I buy something for myself, it's there forever. My records will probably go to the grave with me. You know, there have been times when I've fantasized about owning a record shop. Only trouble is that it would be the kind of shop where people would come in and you'd say, 'Sorry, but nothing is for sale.' "

Labatt's collection is literally world-class, drawn from anywhere he needed to hunt those records down. But it's possible to be among the most diehard collectors, and get it all in one city. By that standard, a guy like Boston-area resident George "Rocky" Stone can take his place at the head of the class. Summing up the extent of his passion is easy. Suffice to say that he works in a record warehouse for a living, a huge hangar-like place with supplies of CDs in every corner, and that his own apartment is even more record-intensive than that. If you can quantify your vinyl obsession by how much of your personal space you're willing to crowd with the stuff, then Rocky has few equals.

Looking around the place, I am truly amazed. It's about the same size as most one-bedroom apartments in the Boston area, not exactly plush but with enough room to keep a bed, a workspace and a little room to stretch out. In this case, however, every available space is taken up by records or CDs: roughly fifteen thousand albums, nearly as many CDs, and a few thousand singles and 78s. They're in the bathroom, too, and his most recently-acquired CDs are stacked on top of the two folding chairs that appear to be the only furniture. At first I assume that he doesn't even have a bed, but I look around some more shelves and I find it—a futon dumped onto six square feet of floor space, bordered on all sides by more shelves. Taped up over the bed are '70s vintage posters of Emmylou Harris and Steeleye Span's Maddy Prior. For someone into country and traditional music, those two are as close to pin-ups as it gets.

And here's the rub: damn near all of those fifty-odd thousand records are desirable. Rocky's jones is for jazz and folk (specifically, English folk-rock), and browsing the discs that reside at eye level, I spot any number of rarities. There's a bootleg of Fairport Convention BBC sessions from the late '60s; over there is a reference CD of rough mixes from Linda Thompson's in-progress (since released) solo album; in another corner I find a trio of collections by an artist I'd lately been discovering, New Orleans bandleader Dave Bartholomew. And there's a couple boxes' worth of recent, unfiled acquisitions that number in the hundreds. This collection is also a model of integration, with the vintage jazz filed right next to the most lilywhite of English traditional. "I don't divide 'em up. That would be like typecasting a person," he explains.

Moving from the dining room to the living room (or to be more accurate, from the record room to the other record room), I encounter still more vinyl, a set heavy on jazz box sets that probably went out of print more than a decade ago. Here I find confirmation for my theory that the most personally telling thing in one's collection is the title of whatever record is placed to catch your eye as soon as you walk into the room. In this case, it's one printed boldly at eye level on the vinyl shelves, a Ray Charles compilation with a four-word title: *A Life in Music*.

"I usually tell people to bring their own smelling salts," he says, as he offers me one of the two folding chairs—not quite all of his furniture, but close. "I do have a couch, but it's buried over there," he says, pointing to another small cove behind shelving. None of the rooms have more than one functional window, the others are all covered with more shelves. "There used to be two windows in the bedroom when I moved in," he notes. "I can't have people staying over here, because there's no place for them to stay." Got to admit that the place feels homey. It reminds me of my old college radio station, which also had the cramped clubhouse feel of too many records (and one control board, and usually some pizza crusts or somebody's missing bong) crammed into too small a space. I loved that room, but then, save for one night when I got locked out of my dorm, I never had to sleep in it.

Graying and bespectacled, Rocky has the slightly disheveled look of a post-grad student who's just put in a few all-nighters. He got the first of many record-store jobs in the '70s, and he now works in the warehouse of the roots-music stronghold Rounder Records. Barring the label owners, he may well be the only person there who can venture an opinion about every damn record in the catalog, which now numbers in the thousands. But his vinyl junkiedom is partly a souvenir from his late-'60s days hanging out in folk clubs, which tend to be basement-size rooms crammed full of people, devoted to the idea of much music in a small space. (Passim in Harvard Square is famously known as the room where Bob Dylan and Joan Baez hung out in the '60s, and you've seen bigger doctor's offices.) Take into account lots of good memories stemming from those years, add a natural inclination to acquire stuff, and let it grow for a few decades in a city full of used record stores . . . next thing you know, you've got fifty thousand albums in a one-bedroom apartment.

"I've listened to everything in here at least once—twice maybe, depending on the artist. My problem is that I'm a completist; if I start liking somebody's music I'll want to have everything that person did. When I started collecting there weren't a lot of good reference books telling you who played on what, so I'm sure I missed a lot of good ones along the way." He's just discovered the hip '50s satirist Lord Buckley, which gives him a good dozen out-of-print albums he needs to track down.

"The people upstairs think I'm a little crazy," he admits. "But most people just say, 'Hey, enjoy yourself.' The only problem is when you start realizing how much you just spent. I've had to put off paying certain bills because some record store would have a sale. At least with this, you have something to show for your money." Even when faced with the dreaded question about the ability to hear all of one's records in the remainder of a lifetime, he takes things in stride. "Certainly not at my age, when the average length of an LP is over 30 minutes. You can only listen to so much at a time, and you can't go playing three LPs at once. But you do what you can. I do have little markers in my CDs for the last time I listened to them."

On my way out the door, I ask once again why he'd want to own so many records. "Well, it's also sort of an archive, like a lending library," he says. That one stops me in my tracks. "You mean you actually lend these things out?" "Sure, go ahead." Turned loose in the proverbial candy store, I scoop up all the Richard Thompson bootlegs and New Orleans jazz I can find, ready to crank my overworked CD burner up long into the night. I'm snobbish enough to think that I'll never be quite as far-gone as Rocky, and that I couldn't imagine being crowded out of my space by a collection that big. But if I use slimline CD cases, I'm sure I can make room for about thirty-two discs worth of it.

Chapter Fourteen

THE ULTIMATE FIND

*M*onoman *is* on the verge of starting an international incident. I'm having a beer at the local rock club, the Middle East, when I spot him down the bar, rifling through a stack of envelopes and gesticulating a little more wildly than usual. He grabs his beer, sits next to me and tells the whole, tragic story. Not long ago, he located one of the records he'd been questing after for years, a record that—in terms of music, history and rarity value—rates as one of his personal Holy Grails. When a collector in Brussels finally offered him a copy, he stashed two thousand and two dollars in cash into an envelope and sent it off to Belgium. That was on the twenty-fifth of May. It's now the fourth of July. Monoman is pissed.

"I'm gonna get the American government involved," he swears. "I sold a lot of really good records to some collector to raise that cash." So maybe, he admits, he shouldn't have just stuck a wad of bills into a registered letter and sent it abroad, but the excitement of locating a prime find was just too strong. "I've talked with the U.S. postal inspectors, and I know when the letter left JFK. I've talked with the Belgian authorities, and I told them you can't put a price on this thing. The letter has not been released to the sendee, so I have not been ripped off by the dealer. It has to be one of the Belgian authorities—hey, they're just a knife-wielding, arms-dealing country, anyway. Is this what a nutcase guy has to do to get his hands on a rare record? Yeah, it really is. Two thousand dollars. So I'm hurting right now, but hopefully we'll prevail."

The object of his affections is Tony Jackson's "Understanding," a four-song EP that is indeed one of the rarest British Invasion artifacts from the '60s. Jackson was the first of the Searchers's lead singers—that's him on their hit version of "Love Potion #9"—and apparently partied too hard for a band with such a clean-cut image. After the Searchers showed him the door, he cut this disc of other people's hits. In addition to the title song, originally done by the Small Faces, there are tunes by the Byrds and Paul Revere & the Raiders. And Monoman knows his British Invasion well enough to tell when he's got something amazing.

"It only came out in Lisbon, Portugal; on Estudio Records," he reports. "Tony Jackson was one of the first British Invasion guys to go solo; and he was the first to get a nose job—as soon as he left the Searchers, he went and got one.

All his records are totally brilliant. It's really less British Invasion than freakbeat. [In other words, it has a strong tinge of psychedelic punk.] You only hear about it being offered for sale once every twenty years or so. In this case, my collector in Brussels went to Lisbon, hit the record fairs and did all the dirty work."

Even if he has to call in the CIA, I have no doubt that he will get his hands on this record. What will he do with this gem when it arrives? "Just own it. I'll only play it when I'm completely drunk, but I'm not gonna break it. There is a certain category of records that sound better the more buzzed you are. There's a Viennese group called the Slaves that's like that, and Tony Jackson definitely is. It's precise but loose at the same time, absolutely wonderful. Records you only play at those times. They'll transport you to a beer-drinking, stupid nirvana the way no other band can." While I've yet to hear any of Tony Jackson's solo efforts, at least Monoman just explained one reason why I love his own band, the Lyres.

I was stone-cold sober the day I turned up one of the peaks on my own must-have list, and maybe that was why it was such an anticlimax. I'd worked for years to find "Atunde," a little-known 45 by the renowned Cream drummer Ginger Baker. The song had already been playing in my imagination for a good two decades: It came out in 1971, about two years after Cream dissolved. Baker had already made two spotty albums with a jazz/rock conglomerate he'd called the Airforce, then he unleashed this obscure single on the world.

Credited to the Ginger Baker Drum Choir, it reflected the African funk he'd then been exploring. But unlike the big-band arrangements his influence Fela Kuti was known for, Baker's single contained nothing but drums and voices—lots and lots of each, to judge from the massive sound it made over my little portable radio.

To my twelve-year-old ears, it was a beautiful, powerful sound: Grownups who'd explored jazz might have been more familiar with this kind of music, but I'd never heard anything like it. For starters, there was that incredibly sensual pulse of the drummers—maybe ten or fifteen, playing at full velocity for four minutes. Then there were the harmonies laid on top—an odd mix of African chant, American gospel and Beatles pop (the lead voice sounded female and very English, as if Dusty Springfield had somehow infiltrated Fela's crew). What's more, the record seemed to change shape every time I heard it on the radio (and yes, it was on the radio: New York's WNEW-FM, now one of a million corporate sound-alike stations, was then the East Coast's premier underground outlet). For the first handful of spins, the lyrics were all in an African tongue. Then, suddenly, English lyrics appeared out of the mix: "We are here—Everything—Is all right!" To make it more perfect, it was released about a month before I grad-uated junior high; and the song's triumphant mood was ex-actly what I was feeling at the time. It was my own personal version of Alice Cooper's "School's Out," which would hit the airwaves a year later.

Instead of buying the 45 when I could have, I taped it on my portable Magnavox cassette machine; both the tape and the machine died maybe six months later—not that I gave it much thought at the time, probably being too busy listening to Alice Cooper. But I carried "Atunde" around in my head all along, until I realized one day that I hadn't heard the thing for a good decade and didn't have a copy. So I set out looking, maybe not too seriously, since I never kept a formal want list and was usually too busy with whatever current passion was on my mind. But I looked for "Atunde" in dozens of stores in at least seven states, with no luck. And I finally redoubled my efforts after a Baker compilation, *Do What You Like*, came out in 1997 and still didn't include the song, which has yet to make it either to album or CD.

When it finally turned up, it didn't even set me back too much: Ten bucks plus postage, from a store registered with the Internet site gemm.com. (Last I checked, you could still buy a more beat-up copy for as little as five.) And I got mine a week later, a nice clean promo copy, where I finally learned the proper title and punctuation ["Atunde! (We Are Here)"— Parts One and Two]. That also solved the lyrical mystery, since the first part was largely African and the second English. I played it right away, and it was . . . still a good record. A really good record, one that sounded pretty much the way I remembered it, although my ears could now pick out some of the separate drum parts instead of hearing it all as one big, overwhelming clatter. Only trouble is that I own so damn many good records by now, and this is just another one. I played it a few times and filed it away. Glad to know it's in my collection, and I'll stick it on a mix tape someday, but I haven't touched it a whole lot since.

The real stars of my collection are records I don't even play that often. I don't collect autographed albums, but I treasure a copy of the Beach Boys's *Smile*—a bootleg approximation of the unfinished 1967 masterwork that famously gave Brian Wilson a nervous breakdown—that I had Wilson sign after an interview. (He stood absolutely still and stared at it for a good forty-five seconds. Just when I was convinced that I'd sent him back to the sandbox, he signed it and handed it back.) Throwing Muses, a band I dearly loved in the '80s, released an EP on their own Blowing Fuses label before anyone had heard of them. What's notable is that the bandmembers colored every picture sleeve themselves with crayons. The sleeve was oversized, so it was a real challenge to keep it in good shape as I packed my collection up for various apartment moves, but it's still intact (even if the band, at this writing, isn't). And I got my third prize from sheer luck: another bootleg, *Ten of Swords* by Bob Dylan, turned up at a local record show about a week before *Rolling Stone* wrote about it, causing Dylan's label to give chase. Price of the ten-album box promptly went up from the seventy-five dollars I paid to about three hundred dollars before it disappeared altogether.

Getting your ultimate find can be a tricky business. Mike Gent, frontman of the excellent New York state band, the Figgs, decided he wanted to own a vinyl copy of every album by one of his favorite bands, the Replacements—easy enough, you'd think, since the Replacements broke up in 1991, just around the time when CDs had completely replaced vinyl.

That means that all their albums were easy to get, except one: *All Shook Down*, their swan song, whose vinyl edition was released only for a short time in Germany. "I hunted that thing down all over the world," says Gent, who made a few trips to Europe on Figgs tours. He was on his honeymoon when he finally uncovered it, filed under "U.S. Indie Rock" at a London shop. "I thought that's it, finally the end of my record shopping. I got what I want and I can now retire. The copy did look a little weird, though—the first side is supposed to have six songs, but there were only five grooves on it. It made me a little curious, but I tried not to think about it too much until I got home." When he did, he put the album right on the turntable and heard what he had. The second side was still the Replacements, but the first was Kenny Rogers & Dolly Parton—a double bill from hell, thanks to a pressing plant screwup. "It's probably good that I didn't figure it out sooner. It would have ruined my honeymoon."

Thurston Moore was once in a situation where one of his most-wanted records was there for the asking, but he couldn't bring himself to ask. "I got pretty involved with collecting avant garde jazz and classical records. [Free jazz drummer] Milford Graves made one I've been looking for, for years—a record that he and [pianist] Don Pullen recorded live at Yale University. There were a couple of those, but the first one had a handpainted sleeve and Graves put it out himself. He's not only one of the foremost purveyors of free jazz, but a herbologist who has a basement full of skeletons and bags of herbs. He's way out in the middle of Queens, and I've driven out there to play duo with him. And I kept thinking, 'How can I ask him for one of those records?' I never did, I just couldn't bring myself to do it." Another rare record that Moore couldn't get was in the house of a musician friend, ex-Minutemen bassist Mike Watt, whose collecting habits are a bit unusual. "Mike has some amazing records in his house, things from the American punk underground. I saw the single by the Huns, and by [ex-Black Flag singer] Henry Rollins's first band. And they're lying around his house, unsleeved and getting chomped on. So I take the Rollins single and I say, 'Mike, you've got to let me have this.' And he said 'No, that's my record.' I said, 'Do you listen to it?' and he said, 'No, man. I can't listen to other dudes' music.' "

Steve Hochman, a music critic for the *Los Angeles Times,* is also a lifelong Beatles fan who's acquired such exotica as an 8-track tape of John and Yoko's *Wedding Album,* and a poster for the official Beatles ice cream bar (the bars themselves remain elusive, or maybe just digested). But he didn't know he already had one of his ultimate finds until it was gone. "I was in second grade when the Beatles first came to America, and I asked my mom to buy me a Beatles album. I went to school that day, came home and saw what she'd bought— one of those soundalike albums, *The Beatles Beat* by the Buggs. It had a cover that looked sort of like *Meet the Beatles,* and it had their versions of 'I Wanna Hold Your Hand' and 'She Loves You,' plus a bunch of songs that weren't even

Beatles songs. Of course I was sorely disappointed—I was seven, but I was old enough to know it wasn't the real thing. I still played it, but it was just something that I had to settle for."

Years later, when Hochman was in college and owned more than his share of real Beatles music, he realized that bargain-bin quickies like *The Beatles Beat* had become the real collectibles, the kind of oddball records that sum up the feel of a time and place. "The great thing about it was, it was so wrong it was right." So he went to pull it out of the closet, and found that his mom had let him down again: She'd sold it years ago at a yard sale. "I started keeping an eye out for it, and it finally turned up at a little store in Santa Barbara, not far from where I grew up. While I was paying for it, I took a close look and realized it wasn't just the same record: I was buying back the very same copy." Thus Hochman was reunited with the first record he ever owned, truly getting back to where he once belonged.

Musician and songwriter Peter Holsapple, of the dB's and the Continental Drifters, has been collecting since childhood, and still holds onto his first copies of Big Star's *Radio City* and John Cale's *Paris 1919*. "I keep 'em because they're good," he says. "The first 45 I ever owned was 'Afrikaan Beat' by Bert Kaempfert and his Orchestra on Decca. It was the theme song to a kids' TV show in the NY area. The flip was 'Echo in the Night' and I was thrilled. I'm not sure what it meant to me exactly, but I was rockin' at four." His big prize to

date is a signed Captain Beefheart record, bought at a yard
sale Beefheart's drummer held. Meanwhile, his own records
are high on other people's want lists. Half the albums by the
dB's have been out-of-print collectibles for years. "I wish 'em
luck, but I don't object to people taping or burning each
other CDs. It's way past the point of my getting paid for it
anyhow."

Sure, it's an accomplishment to track down the stars of your
want list, but sometimes, to quote that great philosopher,
Lemmy of Motorhead, the chase is better than the catch. So
maybe people like Steve Wynn are doing us collectors a favor. As a member of the Dream Syndicate, and later as a
soloist, Wynn's made a few handfuls of albums that are well
appreciated by lovers of neo-psychedelia and quality songwriting. But the most desirable of the lot, from a collector's
standpoint, is the first single from his pre-Dream Syndicate
band, the Suspects, which included future alt-country figure Russ Tolman (of True West) and the Dream Syndicate's
bassist Kendra Smith, later a mysterious and reclusive figure.
Normally quite accommodating to his fans, Wynn's been
asked about the disc's whereabouts often enough over the
years, and he knows damn well where it is: it's sitting in his
father's basement. And it's not moving.

"There's at least fifty copies in there," he admits. "People
will talk to me about that record, but I think it's the worst
thing I've ever done. I won't let it out because I don't want
people to have it. And if it were up to me I'd buy up all the

copies on eBay. There were only six hundred copies to begin with. We probably sent twenty to press and radio and sold one hundred and fifty of them to friends." As a fan of Neil Young and Bob Dylan, Wynn can appreciate the idea of catching a favorite artist in an unguarded moment—just not this particular one of his own. "I've even had people from the fan network offering to fence the record for me, but I'm keeping them. I figure I'll do my part for the collector's market by holding onto the copies I've got."

Still, being a record collector is like searching for the perfect relationship: you like to think that there's something out there that will change your life as soon as you find it. George Carlin used to do a routine about a drug that was so potent, it was "no-poke shit": you wouldn't even have to use it. You'd just score once and stay high, knowing it was in the closet. There's no point collecting records unless you really believe that there's a vinyl equivalent—a record so powerful that you don't have to play it, you can just get a fix from its very presence.

Jeff Gold of Los Angeles owns a record that would probably perform that feat for many collectors. Gold's twenty-five-year career in the music business is enviable enough on its own. After working behind the counter at the Rhino Records store in Santa Monica, he worked himself up to become assistant to the president at A&M Records (where he endeared himself to collectors by dreaming up limited-edition releases, notably that cool 10-inch Squeeze EP), and then moved on to become second in command at Warner Brothers. He's now a full-time record dealer, maintaining a collectibles site at recordmecca.com.

Through all those years, his enduring passion was Jimi Hendrix. As a teenage Hendrix fan, he first made the jump from liking music to collecting it. In 1971, there were only three American Hendrix albums to collect, but there were all sorts of nifty variations you could seek out if you were intrepid enough. "I guess it came from baseball card collecting, which I was also into—there was this treasure-hunt mentality, this pioneering spirit. Nobody had put together the fact that there were all these Hendrix variations, so I was being a pioneer on some level. The original Reprise albums had that original, three-color label—pink, yellow and reddish. I'd discover the difference between the first pressing, the second pressing, the Capitol record club versions. The English ones had laminated covers and higher quality pressings." And of course there was *Electric Ladyland*, which had the solarized photo of Hendrix on the American version, but that sleek, laminated photo of the naked women on the English one.

Gold has owned dozens of copies of *Electric Ladyland* over the years, and one of them is his prize. On one level it's the most useless item in his whole collection: it's the original English copy, the cover worn to crap, the vinyl a mess of fingerprints and scratches, the whole thing practically unplayable. There's even a hint of teeth marks on the cover. Yet this copy outclasses all others, because—fanfare, please—Hendrix used to own it. He made the scratches. There's even a photo to prove that he also did the teeth marks.

"When I opened the cover of that *Electric Ladyland*, out fell two snapshots of him holding the record up; you see both sides of the nude cover and his teeth biting into it. And you start looking at the imperfections on the sleeve and sure enough, there is one very big one right there. I got the impression that the record would be totally destroyed, and in fact it was. I can't possibly clean it, those are Hendrix's fingerprints." And he's got another record from the Hendrix library with something even rarer: a couple of drops of the master's blood. According to Kathy Etchingham—Hendrix's girlfriend from the Experience years, who first put the records up for sale—he cut his hand on a wineglass while playing Bob Dylan's *Highway 61 Revisited*; those same drops are now clogging up the grooves of the copy Gold owns. "I mean, I've got Hendrix's DNA. I could probably clone him."

If ever you'd expect a record to levitate or glow in the dark, this would be the one. In fact, it just sits there on the shelf with the rest of his collection, but it does approach that Carlin ideal of generating a buzz without being used. "I figure that getting Hendrix's records is as close to his mojo as you can ever get."

In all, he's got twenty-six of Hendrix's records (the Experience Music Project in Seattle, official keeper of the legacy, has the rest), and the set didn't cost as much as one would expect. He got them from an online auction from Bonham's in England, and after "a couple of middle-of-the-night bidding sessions," claimed them for $1800. And Hendrix evidently tore through his record collection with the same passion that he tore through his life: out of the twenty-six records Gold has, only one is anything near playable. That's a long-deleted album by the Norwegian psychedelic band, the Dream, which includes an obvious tribute song, "Hey Jimi." Gold notes that "It's signed by their guitarist Terje Rypdal [later a New Age artist of some renown] and it says, 'With all the respect we can give a fellow musician, we dedicate "Hey Jimi" to you.' And out of all the records in his collection, this is the only one that isn't completely totaled. So I don't know what he thought of the Dream, but then again, he kept it."

The contents of a musical icon's record collection can often be a surprise. If you've been to Graceland, you've seen the pieces of Elvis Presley's collection that are on display there, and nearly all of it is what you'd expect Elvis to listen to. There's some gospel, some vintage country, some R&B, and since Elvis had gone to Vegas, there's a live Tom Jones LP. But there's one ringer in the collection: The Allman Brothers Band's *Beginnings*, a mid-'70s reissue of their first two albums. For my money, that was the big mystery: was Elvis a closet Allmans fan? Given a couple more years and sharp enough management, would he have jammed with Dickey Betts and gone down the Southern rock road, as Hank Williams Jr. did?

The Hendrix collection that Gold inherited includes a similar ringer, one album that doesn't quite fit in with your preconceptions about Hendrix. Most of it certainly does: he owned records by the Beatles, a batch of Dylan, Wes Montgomery's guitar landmark *A Day in the Life*, and a load of blues—Muddy Waters's *Real Folk Blues*, Robert Johnson's *King of the Delta Blues Singers*, some Howlin' Wolf and John Lee Hooker. Then there's the one that doesn't quite belong: Bill Cosby's *Revenge*, which according to Gold is just as worn-out as the rest of the pile. We all know how much inspiration Hendrix took from Wolf and Dylan, but did he spend just as much time grooving on Cosby's story about storing a snow-ball in the fridge to whack the neighborhood bully in the summer, finding out his mom threw the snowball away, and then spitting on the guy instead? The mind boggles.

If there's a god of record collecting, he or she has laid a finger on Gold, who's had more lucky accidents than one should be allowed. Not a lot of people, for instance, would be driving through Hollywood with a Dave Edmunds single in their trunk—especially not in 1974, when only a handful of staunch Anglophiles even knew who Edmunds was, let alone what he looked like—and then spot the man himself, talking to Ringo Starr outside the Sunset Strip hotspot, the Roxy. "I'm leaving Tower Records down the street, there's a traffic jam, and I see them standing outside. And the record I have is this incredibly rare single by his first band, Love Sculpture. I park my car, go up to Dave and ask him to sign it, and both our heads are shaking at the probability of this ever happening." Balancing the experience was the fact that Ringo was a bit of a jerk, or at least not keen on being up-staged by a relative unknown. "All he said was, 'No man, I'm not signing tonight.' So that's one autograph I never got."

Even more unlikely was Gold's tale of scoring the rarest non-Hendrix album he's got. Imagine being on vacation in

Australia, hiring a taxi to drive you through a wild animal park to see kangaroos, and mentioning casually that you collect rare records. The driver says, "You ought to visit my friend, he's got some great blues records." Most of us would ditch the guy as soon as possible, but Gold rode a hunch. "It's five-thirty, I'm exhausted, but I figure I'd humor the guy, so I tell my wife I'll be a half-hour late. But it turns out his friend was an advertising copywriter who'd lived in America in 1962 and made friends with Muddy Waters and Howlin' Wolf. So I'm starting to think that this could be interesting." What he found in the pile was an early album by Delta bluesman Frank Frost, one of the rarest blues albums in the world. "Who'd imagine that I'd find this thing in Australia? The record was produced by (Sun Records honcho) Sam Phillips, it was pressed on his own Phillips International label, and for some reason it never came out. The albums are all a little off-center. The guy asks me what it's worth and I said, 'Thousands of dollars.' He said, 'Good, you can keep looking,' as if he knew I wasn't going to bullshit him." What followed was an hour of driving through town to pull the requisite four grand from various Melbourne cash machines. Suffice to say he was late for dinner.

What do you do with a four-thousand-dollar album? You play it. "Absolutely. I don't understand people who can buy really expensive records and never touch them. To me it's the same as having a first-edition book: you've got an artifact from the time that it was made, and to me it's got a lot more presence. You're hearing it the way somebody would have heard it at the time, albeit on a much better stereo."

It may be a little sobering to realize that one of the most valuable records in the world, one that you'd trash an Australian vacation for, is still only worth a few grand, not even enough to get you a decent used car. Never mind rational judgment, however: whether it's Tony Jackson's back pages, Steve Wynn's fledgling attempts, or Hendrix's teeth marks, there are some things you can't put a price on.

Chapter Fifteen

THE SOUNDTRACK of YOUR LIFE

*F*or some collectors, it's not just about acquiring a bunch of records. It's about living in the pop culture era of your choice. Anyone who gets deep into non-standard music is already making a decision about living outside the mainstream. If you discovered punk rock in high school, you were differentiating yourself from the Bon Jovi masses. And if you collect jazz, blues or '60s psychedelia, you're sending a message—at least to yourself— that you've evolved beyond the constraints of pop culture. And while you're at it, you can always acquire a bunch of records.

Peter Prescott is the type who wouldn't be caught dead living in the mainstream. Among the Boston music community, he's known as a gifted drummer and a founding member of the post-punk band Mission of Burma (who influenced the likes of the Replacements and Sonic Youth; got covered by R.E.M. and Moby; and broke up in the early '80s, but recently did a successful reunion tour). He's also known as the town cynic: at the Burma show I saw, he punctured the event quite nicely by greeting the crowd with an exaggerated, "It's so nice to see so many wonderful old faces!" When not on tour, he manages a funky basement of a record store in the pricey Newbury Street area; the kind of place that seems to exist as an antidote to its surroundings. I spent an hour there recently, and didn't see anybody buy anything. But we did get through both sides of a European, red-vinyl pressing of the Cramps's *Flamejob*, which he threw on the turntable as soon as a used-vinyl dealer brought it into the store. Instead of skipping over the song "Let's Get Fucked Up," as they would surely have done at Tower or Virgin if they played the album at all, Prescott just turned the volume up a tad.

If he maintains a bit of ironic distance about reunion tours, he feels the same way about collecting. "I've never had much patience for people who treat records like diamonds," he says after we adjourn to a nearby coffeehouse. "Of course, I can see why you'd treat them that way, if you'd paid $150 for a record, but I can't imagine doing that either. Some people collect records the way people collect statues, Beanie Babies—that's their approach to the world. If you want to fill your house with newspapers or thimbles, go ahead. But it's a lot easier for me to relate to someone who collects something with an aesthetic value beyond its collectibility. Collecting is like a prism, a lot is what you project onto it. For some it satisfies an obsessive-compulsive-disorder-style need. And if that keeps people from going nuts, more power to them. Most collectors, in an honest moment, would admit there's a pathetic side to it—it's an obsessive need for an object, which is pretty pathetic. But it doesn't have to be only that."

What it can be, for him, is a personal version of the do-it-yourself ethic: program your own music instead of letting the culture do it for you. "I don't think I've changed my mode of dress very much since I was 25," says Prescott, now into his 40s with a preference for jeans, T-shirts and punkish, close-cropped hair. During that time, his musical taste has only become more idiosyncratic. Along with punk rock, he's developed a love for the experimental rock of the Birthday Party and the Fall, and the "space age bachelor pad" realm of '60s easy-listening.

"Now that I've owned up to being a collector, I'll say that what really gets me off is knowing I have this personal library of everything that appeals to me, and that I can pull any of it out whenever I want to. That's the wonderful thing, customizing the soundtrack of your life. It goes against the fact that so many things are considered disposable now. Music has always been the center of my life, and to some extent it keeps you from just walking outside and fitting into the crowd. What better way to avoid that than to surround yourself with the music that you relate to the most? That really is a way of adjusting the world to you."

But some specialty collectors have evolved even further, taking themselves to a particular corner of pop history, usually a particular corner of the '60s—always a rich era for pop culture. Since many collectors are in their 30s and 40s, they just missed growing up in that era, so they see it as something of a lost paradise. But that doesn't mean you can't absorb the music, and shape a bit of your worldview accordingly. Maybe you can't transport yourself back to the days of the British Invasion, or to the Sunset Strip in 1966, or to Las Vegas when Frank and Dino were around. But at least you can bask in a little bit of that glory.

In this realm, it's often the female collectors who can be a little more creative with their personal style, and a whole lot more creative with their choice of a musical soundtrack. High on the list would be Lisa Sutton, a Los Angeles-based artist and designer who finds a source of inspiration in her lifelong passion for bubblegum.

She's an easy one to spot in a crowd, especially this crowd. It's a county fair in Newport, Rhode Island, and the entertainment is provided by the most famous group to come out of this city, the Cowsills, the singing family that scored a few quintessential bubblegum hits in the '60s. And this corner of Newport looks pretty much the same as it did when "Indian Lake" was on the radio. It's still a place where the yachters hang out. Today it's a suntanned, mostly well-to-do crowd heavy on porkpie hats and shirts with little anchors on them—in all, the atmosphere is more lobster roll than rock 'n' roll. Having reunited and recorded over the past decade, the Cowsills are now appreciated by power-pop diehards, but that's not who's in this crowd: it's the old Newport locals and the middle-aged rockers who still cherish their teen crushes on various Cowsill sibs. Lisa is here to interview them for a VH1 documentary—at the moment, she knows more dirt on the group than anyone outside the immediate family—and she stands out in this company. She's the one with the TV cameras and the purple hair.

I think of Lisa as the grown-up version of those girls you'd see in cartoons in teen magazines—the ones dancing around their room with the radio on, cutting photos of their favorite pin-up. You figured they'd grow up to be funky and artsy, and she has. An artist and occasional TV producer, she personifies the Huey Lewis law of nature—namely, it's hip to be square. The purple hair attests to her days as a punk rocker and *Rocky Horror* devotee. But her abiding love is for bubblegum, music that is some of the least hip and most fun in pop history. Her work in the biz has helped keep that era alive: She's compiled and annotated various Bobby Sherman and Brady Bunch compilations. The first thing I learned about her was that she's re-painted a Monkees album cover. The original prints for *Pisces, Aquarius, Capricorn & Jones Ltd* are long gone, so when the album was reissued in the '80s she created a lookalike cover (if you bought it since then, you've got her version) and I can pride myself on being one of the few dozen people in the world who would be impressed by that. In another life, she might have been Keith Partridge's girlfriend. But her personal soundtrack connects her to a place where the '60s are still in progress, and everybody's having a nice day.

"I was born in a constant state of nostalgia," she explains—a line she borrowed from songwriter Rupert Holmes, but one that she can wear proudly. "I'll admit that I totally pine for the '60s; it's something about those earlier, wonderful, carefree days. My father used to go to parties in Topanga, and I remember being a kid and really wanting to go to Woodstock [which wasn't likely to happen, since she was seven that summer]. But it was so beautiful to live in L.A. at that time, surrounded by the whole hippie culture. It wasn't about replacing anything that was missing in my life, but when I grew up I wanted to get one of everything I'd ever wanted as a kid. And if having one or two Partridge Family records meant a lot to you once, then having them all would mean even more."

I suggest that her musical taste might be a hard sell to other collectors—even with my abiding love for the Monkees and Cowsills, I'm reluctant to follow her into Partridge territory. "I just think it means that I dig really good pop music, since I also like things like the Free Design and Association [two equally frothy, but more critically sanctioned bands]. But the Partridges were probably easier to get into, after the teenage crush I had on David Cassidy." And it's not that much of a contradiction that she was equally drawn to the innocent world of the Partridges and the less innocent one of *Rocky Horror*. "It's really on the same level, the glam and the glitz. When you're a kid you respond to color, same way that they're into the whole tie-dye thing now. But the '60s were the last time when that whole kind of grooviness was going on. Back then it was cool to want to be a go-go dancer, and nowadays that would make you a stripper."

In fact, a teenage life crisis turned her into a born-again bubblegummer. "The only way to describe it is that I was the victim of a random act of violence. I was in eleventh grade, and I was beaten up badly by a girl in my school—bruised and battered so badly that my mother didn't want me leaving the house. This girl was looking for a fight with someone, and she just whomped me. My right eye was paralyzed. It was horribly depressing. Then a friend came over while I was laid up, and she brought a copy of *The Partridge Family Sound Magazine*—I'd owned that when I was younger, but now I was a teenager and it just wasn't cool anymore. That was a ritual when you were growing up, you'd reach a certain age and get rid of those records. You'd sell them for a buck-fifty and throw a part of your childhood away.

"So now my friend comes over with the Partridge Family, and I had a real emotional reaction. We put it on, sat there and sang and laughed, and I just loved the hell out of that record. This was around the time they started re-running the Monkees on MTV, and after not having seen it for so many years, I watched it and just got tears in my eyes. From there we started going to used record stores, buying Monkees and Partridge Family albums for a buck. That was when I started record collecting. And I still think that *The Partridge Family Sound Magazine* is one of the finest albums ever recorded."

Though it started on impulse, her collection's become amazingly thorough. She's got actual boxes of Rice Krispies with teen idols' faces on them, and the krispies still inside. She's got David Cassidy necklaces, many stacks of coloring books and paper dolls, and every issue of *Tiger Beat* that's come out since 1965. Her memorabilia regularly gets leased to magazines and TV shows looking for a little period flavor. The lava lamps and smiley-face clocks that adorned Rhino's *Have a Nice Day* series? Those were Lisa's. So was the poster spread of Monkees ephemera that came with their box set— an array of Monkees clocks, posters, puzzles, trading cards and the odd tambourine, even a copy of the very "Monkees Music Book" that I learned to play guitar out of when I was ten. Damn, I'd been looking for that one myself.

But her love for the Partridge Family has been the biggest springboard to her collecting. And yes, one can be serious about collecting a group that never literally existed. Her personal Holy Grail was a set of records she's heard about before she actually saw them: acetates that were produced for the cast members, so they could learn the songs and lip-sync them onscreen. "Collectors refer to them as the Screen Gems records, or the rehearsal records. There were three or four of these for every season of the show—they each have an album version of the song, plus the short TV version, and maybe an alternate version as well. If they weren't owned by one of the six cast members, they would come from the musical supervisor, or the director of that episode. To me that's the pinnacle of cool—to have these records and be pretty much the only person that has them, as sick as that sounds." Especially since the copies she eventually found, and spent a total of two grand to get, came from a garage sale at Tracy Partridge's—that's actress Suzanne Crough's—house.

"My mother used to tell me that I did everything to excess," she notes. "I think it's true that it's largely a male thing, that hunter/gatherer mentality. Girls are more inclined to think about things like, well, David Cassidy's hair. When you find women that are big time collectors, it's usually that they're more aggressive types; girls don't have that mentality as much as men do. But I also think that we all have that drive, we all have varying degrees of testosterone in us." Not surprisingly, she says that collectors of teen-idol pop tend to be even more obsessed than the rest of us. "I'm the first to admit that I've met some really odd people in the collecting world. Eighty-five percent are lunatics, and the rest have something wrong with them—they're greedy or competitive, or just not nice. But that's fine, we all have some geekiness in us. And I believe you should let your geek flag fly."

Super-fans devoted to one artist are among the most devoted collectors there are. Beatles collectors are still as rabid as ever, to judge from a recent eBay auction that found the notorious "Butcher cover"—the garish pop-art satire that was quickly yanked from the front of the *Yesterday & Today* album—being snapped up for more than two grand. I know a Bruce Springsteen fan who keeps two copies of every one of the Boss's albums—one to play, the other a sealed copy held in reserve, just in case an artist that popular should suddenly vanish from the shelves. And you've got to hand it to fans of the Grateful Dead (and Phish, and scads of other jam-bands) who managed to collect and catalog endless hours of tapes and bootleg CDs, even while living in a van to follow their heroes on the road.

It's only natural that some of the most admired artists in popular music should have suitably devoted fans. It takes a little more gumption to dedicate yourself to someone who's obscure, overlooked, or just plain unhip. My choice for originality would go to Boston writer Zoe Gemelli, who devoted a good chunk of her life to an artist who's not often mentioned when the usual lists of the all-time greatest come up.

When most young lesbians talk about Olivia Records, they're usually talking about the label of that name; the one that signed the likes of Meg Christian and Cris Williamson, and popularized the notion of "women's music" before Ani, k.d. and the riot grrls came along. But for Zoe, Olivia records were something different: they were Olivia Newton-John's records. They were the ones that took all her money and every available inch of apartment space; the ones that were integral to her escaping her born-again Christian background, finding herself as a writer and coming out as gay. A pretty tall order, you might think, for "I Honestly Love You" and "Have You Never Been Mellow."

To some extent Zoe's life was tangled with Olivia's since day one: That would be September 16, 1971, the day she was born and the week that Olivia's first hit single, the George Harrison cover "If Not For You," was in the charts. As an avid listener of AM radio and reader of teen magazines, Zoe discovered her idol just a few years later. "Why Olivia?" she ponders, probably holding back the impulse to ask "Why not?" "It's so hard to pick one reason. For one thing, I really loved her music and her voice. And on an unconscious level, there was something really wholesome and honest about her. I needed someone to look up to who was *good*. She represented that in the industry as much as anyone, and I was too young to understand punk rock." And nowadays she can justify her taste like the music critic she's become: "You can say that the Patti Smiths of the world are beautifully talented, but people like Olivia and the Spice Girls will make you get up and dance. There's a place in the world for both. And there was a time in my life when I didn't admit my Olivia fondness to anyone. I got over that, though—decided I didn't want to be ashamed of anything in my music collection."

Crushes on artists are a cherished part of the record-collector experience. But having those crushes doesn't necessarily lead to a collecting jones. For heterosexual guys reading '60s teen magazines, the pickings were definitely slimmer. The first strong musical crush I can remember was on a singer calling herself Jennifer, who was a regular on the *Smothers Brothers Show*. A definite hippie dream, Jennifer was prone to white lipstick and peasant dresses, and she wore glasses more fetchingly than Lisa Loeb ever dreamed. I remember her singing "Easy to be Hard" on the show one week, exuding a wide-eyed waifishness that nailed me to the wall, or at least my parents' couch. (I recently lucked into the video of this show and yep, Jennifer and the song are still pretty gorgeous.) But I've still never owned one of the woman's records, even after I put it together, many years later, that she's the same Jennifer Warnes who hit with "Right Time of the Night" and made a critically-praised album of Leonard Cohen songs—it just wouldn't be the same. (My more recent crushes on Kristin Hersh and Liz Phair don't count, they only happened after I was a fan of their music.) My first stabs at record collecting were more like male bonding—I yearned to hang out with people like Mike Nesmith of the Monkees, who was smarter and snottier than anyone else in *16 Magazine*. Or Mark Lindsay of Paul Revere & the Raiders, who seemed a mix of the sensitive type I already was and the party animal I really wanted to be. And he had that really bitchin' Revolutionary War hat.

But Zoe's Olivia phase was a more profound rite of passage. She sustained it over ten years, and it went from cutting pictures out of teen magazines to getting her first record store jobs, bringing home a weekly stash of Olivia booty. Even today, with the spell long since broken, she's quick to head off any cheap shots about her idol's career. How about the movie *Xanadu*, pop culture's first and only linking of Greek mythology and roller disco? "Loved it. To me that's the ultimate fan's film. It has all the right elements of pure kitsch, and the sense of 'Let's milk the fans for everything they've got.' If you can appreciate what the Spice Girls did with *Spiceworld*, then *Xanadu* comes out of the same place." Okay, so what about the long-forgotten hit "Let's Get Physical," and the singer's attempt to recast herself as an edgy sex symbol? "Oh, that was awesome. It made me fall even more in love with her. Suddenly she was everywhere, you could turn on the TV and she'd always be on, and I liked those times when she was more accessible. Besides, the image change wasn't that big a stretch after the end of *Grease*—you look at 'Physical' and it was really just an extension of Sandy II."

Redheaded and bespectacled, Zoe herself evinces a style somewhere between the early, wholesome Olivia and the later, sexy one. As a lesbian in her early 30s, and a recovering Olivia-fan, she doesn't exactly fit the collector stereotype of a middle-aged guy with a Springsteen or Beatles fetish. She met her share of the latter when she was frequenting used-record stores and later working in one herself—the better to enhance her stash of Oliviana. "I can tell you that a lot of the stereotypes are reality. The male collectors are more status-oriented and more into the details; if I didn't know as much as they did, it didn't take long for them to write me off. I didn't get a lot of their respect until I started winning music trivia contests. It was always a challenge to keep up, and it still is."

Yet she caught the fever as strong as anybody, and had thousands of Olivia records to show for it. With an international star who dabbled in disco, there are at least two slippery slopes to go down, and she took both: there were Australian-only singles and European picture sleeves on one hand, limited 12-inch remixes on the other. And that was only the start. "She did *Xanadu* with the Electric Light Orchestra, so there were all the ELO singles I had to get. Then there were a lot of K-tel albums that had only one song by her. There were the cheap albums on the Pickwick label that said 'Sounds Like Olivia Newton-John.' I got those even though they didn't really sound like her." Then there was her French label's habit of putting a special, starburst-type logo on the picture sleeve of any single that made it to #1 in that country—thus Zoe had to find that version of the "I Honestly Love You" 45.

Like all good relationships, hers with Olivia grew and evolved over the years. "I started by cutting out pictures and hanging them on the bedroom wall. They I'd play the records and act out little skits to the songs." As she grew older, the attachment only got more intense: she started listening intently to AM radio and following singles charts, tuning in whenever a Newton-John record was being pitted against someone else's, wondering how she could be beaten out by lesser talents like Elton John and Paul McCartney. Then she got hold of collectors' magazines, finding out just how many of her idol's records were out there in different forms and with different sleeves. There were enough out there to fill up her one-bedroom apartment, as they wound up doing.

"It got a lot easier around the time I started getting a paycheck. Then I started going for the Australian-only albums, the ones that might have a song that hadn't made it to America. There was one album where the cover got changed after the first pressing, that was the one I spent the most money on. Of course I needed them because they were unique; it wasn't something everybody else had. You could always get somebody to tape the songs for you, but it wasn't the same—I just liked knowing that everybody else had the other cover. I wound up owning at least one version of everything she ever released on vinyl. And if she covered somebody else's song, I had to get that artist's album, too. I have an 'Olivia-related' section with a couple hundred singles in it. She made me start buying Peter Allen records, and I didn't think anyone else cared about getting Lesley Duncan's album [in fact a lot of Elton John fans did, because he also covered one of her songs]. It lasted all through my teenage years, and I spent thousands of dollars on her. I remember how hard I cried when I found out she had breast cancer, which was around the time I moved out of my parents' house."

Depending on how many rumors about Olivia Newton-John's sex life you believe, Zoe's choice of a role model might be especially apt. "The rumors that she was gay? Believe it or not, I had a hard time hearing those things. I was in a born-again Christian household at the time, and I wasn't any-where near ready to hear something like that." For what it's worth, Newton-John herself has denied the rumors, which sprang from an appearance on the Johnny Carson show in the '70s. Asked if she'd come to the studio with a date, the singer—who apparently didn't know her American idioms too well—said she'd come with a girlfriend, thus spicing up her image a bit more than intended. "She said it was taken out of context and only she knows if there's anything beyond that, but the rest isn't my business."

Besides, something about first crushes needs to be kept pure. Zoe's actually given serious thought over the years as to whether she'd sleep with Olivia if the chance ever arose— and since she wound up working in the music business, the possibility of at least meeting her wasn't out of the question— and she probably did her own love life a favor by deciding not to go for it. "All of my ex-girlfriends asked about that," she admits. "I confessed all this to my last one; she called me a freak. The funny thing, though, is that my feelings for her never turned sexual, my own sexuality never had much to do with it. What she gave me was more the escape from my home life and the freedom to find myself. I do remember the moment I started having sexual feelings for a woman, and her name was Madonna." When I suggest that other '80s pop stars might have been more crushworthy—say, the androgynous allure of Annie Lennox—she zeroes in on one of Madonna's trade secrets. "The problem is, that if I had felt attracted to Annie Lennox or someone else, that would have been admitting I was homosexual. Madonna was a totally sexual being—everybody loved her and was attracted to her. So it didn't mean anything in particular if I was."

What finally broke the spell was a near-random encounter with one guy who had a bigger Olivia obsession than hers. "It was Claude from Montreal, someone I'd met through the fan club. We were always trying to outdo each other, and I remember him saying, 'I am her number one fan in the world.' Suddenly I just started laughing: what made him believe he could possibly have the right to that title? And I remember what I said—'Her number one fan has to remain her daughter.' Even though I spent every last penny on her, I realized he knew more about her than I ever would; he'd gotten to a level that I didn't want to go to. I wasn't her number one fan and never would be. I walked away and that was it." Thus ended the first great love affair of her life.

Zoe had been through her moment of reckoning by the

time she finally met her heroine at a record-store appearance. "All I said was 'Hi, nice to meet you'—it wasn't a thrilling moment on either of our parts. But it meant I could get on with my life." Still, old loves die hard—she may have purged her Olivia collection, but kept all of the greatest-hits CDs. She was still the only person on her block to buy Newton-John's last CD opus, *Gaia*, and to think it wasn't half bad. "My girlfriend agreed to let me play it as long as we could hear the new Madonna record first." The people that pay her to write about music probably don't know the extent of her Olivia obsession, but she can look back at those days with some amusement. "I don't mind revisiting it, but it's not me anymore. It's become like a joke in some quarters, but I'm proud of where it took me. When it was over I realized I'd grown up." She still wouldn't mind a date with Madonna, however.

CHAPTER SIXTEEN
BONUS TRACK

SIDE B
33⅓

"L*et's talk* about Bowie," Monoman says, taking in the area around him with a wide sweep of his arm. The band onstage is taking a break, and he's just turned the alcove outside the Middle East bathrooms into his private Speaker's Corner.

"Okay, so you agree that those David Jones records he did in 1966 were the best things he ever did, right?" Not quite, but I can see why he would think so: they're wild, garagey records like the kind he makes himself. "Then, of course, he went into his Anthony Newley phase. . . ." He flashes a look of appropriate disgust. "Then, he did that *Space Oddity* one and you probably think it sucks, right?" Not exactly, but after three decades I could live without hearing it again. "Well, you're wrong. It was a brilliant record." A young punk on his way to the stalls hears this discussion and chimes in with the name of a once-prominent British musician. "You mean the guy I did coke with at the Paradise in 1977?" Monoman asks. The kid nods, duly impressed.

"Okay, so what came after *Space Oddity?*" I nod, secure in the view that any beginner knows the answer. "Right. *The Man Who Sold the World.* Great album. The one with that cover . . ." Monoman mimics the Bowie pose on the cover of the American album—kicking his foot high in a modern-dance move, nearly knocking over the same kid on his way out of the bathroom. What he's found has just made his day and re-energized his collecting: the early-'70s reel-to-reel version of that album, which he swears is the best-sounding version that's ever been produced. (Reel tapes, at that time, were struck directly off the album production masters, which were compressed for vinyl. The same masters may be used for modern CDs—but this was nearly twenty years earlier, when the tapes were still throbbing.) For Monoman the tape's easily worth a few hundred, but the buzz he gets from its very proximity is priceless. "The sonics on this are gonna be incredible. And I will continue to acquire more, make no mistake about that. It's life! It's excitement! And it's better than paying bills or buying seedless watermelons for $4.99 at Star Market."

This newfound passion for Bowie, however, is partly his way of rebounding from a heartbreak: his relentless pursuit of Tony Jackson is not paying off. It's been three months since he obeyed an impulse, put two grand cash into an en-

velope, and sent it to Brussels to get a rare EP by the Searchers's original singer. Since then it's been all headaches and no
music. There's no telling who helped themselves to a cash-
filled envelope on which side of the Atlantic; what's certain
is that somebody did. "I've been in touch with the Belgian
postal authorities, Customs at the airport, and they all say
that one word: L–O–S–T. I'm betting it went up somebody's
arm."

But the record is still out there, it's still calling to him, and
only someone with a true heart for collecting will understand
what Monoman's just done: he's spent another two thousand
for the same disc, this time through the dealer's secure PayPal
account. Never mind that he already owns all the music on
this record, having tracked down a bootleg Tony Jackson
CD from Europe. But that's only the music, what he really
needs is to get close to the essence.

Such goals don't come easily: to raise the two grand he
had to liquidate part of his collection and only God (and his
girlfriend) know how many bills went unpaid. "There's a guy
who lives with his mother in a florist shop—he bought one
of my thousand-dollar singles. If I'd known that the guy with
the Tony Jackson record had this PayPal account, I wouldn't
be standing here doing this crybaby thing right now. But
that's how it works. The IRS is on your ass, you might go to
jail, you've got to sell some of your greatest records to pay
the bills. Sometimes you have to do that and, man, it really
hurts. You get hurt, but you have to keep going on. You've
got to keep collecting, and you've got to keep being a fan of
music."

I make a mental note to see if I can find anything by Tony Jackson. Meanwhile, I have to listen to the Tuatara and Minus Five albums that Peter Buck induced me to buy. The Partridge Family reissue CDs that Lisa Sutton induced me to get. The collection of Crumb's favorite 78s that got released in Germany. The Jellyfish box set that I hunted down after talking to Roger Manning. The live CD of a recent tour that Steve Wynn sent me. The thirty-two folk-rock CDs I burned off Rocky Stone's collection. Zoe's Olivia mix tape. And the copy of *Music to Break Any Mood* that Pat assured me would be a chick magnet. Steve Turner didn't send me anything, but made me promise to burn him a copy of an old Ventures CD that he was looking for.

I next encounter Monoman a month later, when he's playing guest DJ at a local rock bar. I make my way back to his table, where he's surrounded himself with an archive of mid-'60s music, mostly CDs of limited, semi-bootleg European and Japanese issue. Outtakes of prominent bands, thirty-song collections by totally obscure ones, even a disc's worth of songs whose artists' identities are lost to history. Not a standard, easily purchasable disc anywhere in his stack.

"Hold on, I'm going to play this one for you," he says, shielding the disc's identity as he heads for the DJ station. He cranks it up and the room gets hit by a wave of pure beat-combo savagery: Tony Jackson. It's the record of his dreams, in his clutches at last. Back at the table, he tells me the whole story again: How Jackson got booted from the Searchers just before they recorded their breakthrough hit, "Needles &

Pins." How Jackson was the first rock figure to get a nose job—he produces an earlier Searchers album cover to point out the before-and-after. Then there's the record in question, four songs recorded at a radio studio in Lisbon right before Jackson broke up his band and gave up on his music career.

I try to listen with proper respect, remembering that this record cost Jeff something like two hundred dollars per minute, during "He Was a Friend of Mine"—a folk song that Jackson borrowed from his contemporaries, the Byrds. It's not quite a revelation, but it's sure not often that one hears an English singer, in a Portuguese studio, singing about John F. Kennedy. Monoman's not talking either, just nursing his drink and nodding his head to say "I told you so." And the next track is indeed the keeper: Jackson's version of "Just Like Me." I already know it's a great song, a close cousin to "Louie Louie," since I grew up with Paul Revere & the Raiders's original. But this is 1965 instead of the Raiders's 1964, and Jackson's band gives it a whole different groove—tougher and more drug-informed, with the same kind of Eastern guitar solo that Jeff Beck used to play in the Yardbirds. "Jeff Beck recommended this guy," Monoman says about the unknown guitarist on the record. "Tony Jackson went after Beck before he was known, and Beck said, 'No, but hire this kid instead.'" I become amazed that the people in the bar can nod their heads and carry on conversations, as if this was any old music they were hearing.

It's the last record of the night; he orders one more Cape Codder and prepares to pack up his stash. As if on cue, one of the waitresses comes up to our table. "The manager really wants to know what that record was that you just played." It's the moment that cost four thousand dollars and four months of headaches. Monoman tries not to gloat too hard.

INDEX